Disowning the Violence

Challenging the disturbing image of
God in the Old Testament

Tina Stubbs

Copyright © 2022 Tina Stubbs

The moral right of the author has been asserted.

Apart from any fair dealing for the purposes of research or private study, or criticism or review, as permitted under the Copyright, Designs and Patents Act 1988, this publication may only be reproduced, stored or transmitted, in any form or by any means, with the prior permission in writing of the publishers, or in the case of reprographic reproduction, in accordance with the terms of licences issued by the Copyright Licensing Agency.
Enquires concerning reproduction outside those terms should be sent to the publishers.

The bible quotations used here are from the New Revised Standard Version Bible Copyright © 1989 by the Division of Christian Education of the National Council of Churches of Christ in the United States of America.

The Listening People
15 Cleeve Grove
Keynsham,
Bristol, BS31 2HF

ISBN 978-1-915288-05-9

British Library Cataloguing in Publication Data.
A catalogue record for this book is available from the British Library.

Why didn't anyone ever tell me this?

Contents

Setting the scene - - - - 1

Part 1: The Problem

1. A very human book - - - 8
2. The violent acts of God - - - 10
3. "Virtuous violence" - - - 27
4. Sexism and discrimination - - - 33
5. Has the bible encouraged violence? - 43
6. Can the violence be justified? - - 47
7. Eroding authority? - - - - 58

Part 2: Building the Picture

1. Where did the bible come from? - - 66
2. Contradictions - - - - 71
3. Is it true? - - - - 78
4. A definition of history - - - 86
5. The chosen people - - - - 88
6. Is suffering a punishment for sin? - 99
7. Great storytellers - - - - 104
8. The Law and the Prophets - - - 110

Part 3: Interpreting the Bible for Today

1. Ideas change - - - - 120
2. Why read the Old Testament? - - 124
3. The next generation - - - 132
4. In summary - - - - - 137
5. Conclusion - - - - - 140

Appendix
How is the bible the "Word of God"? - 146
What others say - - - - 148
Bibliography - - - - - 155

Setting the Scene

Over many years I have been shocked, worried and puzzled by the many violent images of God in the Old Testament. I have met many other people with the same concerns. I also know people who have been completely put off the whole concept of a loving God and Christianity by reading accounts of God's wholesale slaughter. Worse still, people who have never read the bible are negatively influenced by what they believe it says or what other people have told them it teaches.

When I was eleven years old, I had a school teacher who was the most wonderful storyteller. Everyone looked forward to scripture lessons. We cheered for David against Goliath. We "saw" the walls of Jericho come crashing down. We sympathised with the misery of the Israelite slaves. But then came the angel of death, killing the firstborn in every Egyptian family and I imagined all those dead people, including babies… and the soldiers bogged down and drowning in the Red Sea, and I thought: *If God loves everybody, what about them? Did God love the Egyptians? Would God really kill innocent babies?*

As a teenager, I picked up a bible and read the book of Joshua. I was horrified to read that God ordered the murder of the inhabitants of entire cities: men, women, children and animals. They don't put that in the stories for children but it's there and is an integral and significant part of the story. I was certain that could not be true. Because of this I "wrote off" the Old Testament – for years! If only someone had told me that the bible tells what people *thought* about God as much as it tells about God himself and that many horrific acts are attributed to God for which he could never have been responsible.

After many years of reading the bible and books about

it, I worked out a theory about the violence which worked for me. I came to appreciate that the Old Testament as a whole had much to contribute to faith and worship and learned how essential its themes and ideas were to understanding the New Testament. But it is Jesus who gives us the clearer image of God and we must view the Old Testament with this in mind.

Ironically (God does have a sense of humour), it was an experience involving a verse from the disturbing book of Joshua which probably changed the direction of my life! (The whole story comes in part 3 below.)

I continue to have a passionate belief that the stories of God zapping enemies cannot be true. A series of people in bible studies and Sunday schools have found me annoying or a breath of fresh air, depending on their point of view. Realising there are things you do not have to believe can be a great relief!

The magazine, *Big Issue*, has a feature where a well-known person writes a "Letter to my younger self." What follows in this book is the information that I would like to have been given when I was twenty or so years old and having huge issues with the Old Testament, particularly the destructive acts of God, which traditional answers did not satisfy.

I would like to be able to pass this on to anyone who has problems coming to terms with difficult issues in the bible and is looking for answers, especially those who are troubled by the violent nature of God portrayed in much of the Old Testament. There *is* an answer.

I hope that anyone having the same concerns which I grew up with, will find this a useful introduction to a possible solution and that those who do not see a problem might start to reconsider and view the destructive episodes in a different light.

I want to make it absolutely clear that I value the bible and nothing that follows is intended to undermine its importance or anyone's faith. Research has *enhanced* my faith by removing some obstacles and thereby making the bible more understandable and believable. I hope it may be the same for you.

According to the Old Testament, God orders and carries out spectacular acts of violence. *My object is to show that the way we interpret the bible as a whole gives us permission to discount the truth of this destructive and cruel image of God.*

The route we follow

We begin by seeing the bible as a human book, which God adopts and uses. We acknowledge the huge importance of the bible and see Jesus and his life and teaching as the lens through which we need to view the world and other parts of the bible.

Chapters 1 to 4 describe examples of God's supposed violence as described in the Old Testament, in war, harsh punishments, racism, sexism, other discrimination and praise of violent acts, to illustrate how extensive and shocking the problem is. Following each example, we contrast the actions with those of Jesus. We consider the need to "read against the grain" and other ways of seeing the violence objectively.

Chapter 5 gives examples of how, throughout history, a literal interpretation of many bible stories has been used to justify and encourage violence.

Chapter 6 outlines attempts that have been made to justify God's supposed violent acts.

Chapter 7 addresses the issue of biblical authority.

In part two we explore a range of topics, which considered together, build up a way of interpreting and understanding the bible which allows us to discount the truth of God's violent behaviour.

We examine:

1. How the bible came to us: writing, editing, compiling, translating, involving debate and controversy.

2. Examples of contradictions, repetitions and mistakes. More evidence of a very human process.

3. Is it True? Different kinds of truth and finding truth expressed in stories and myths.

4. Is it Historical? Definitions and interpretations of history. Did it really happen?

5. The Chosen People: How the Israelites wrote and interpreted their history. Or was it theology? Or was it politics?

6. Examples of very different and contrasting views expressed by biblical authors. What is the nature of God and what does he value? Some core Israelite beliefs challenged within the bible.

7. What is our image of God? How the story is told influences our perceptions.

8. We see the huge importance placed on the Law, and review some positive aspects and the different approaches of the prophets.

Throughout, we see the Old Testament as a product of its time, place, culture and consequent belief systems.

Part three looks at the positive side of the Old Testament and its relevance for today.

We see the bible as a "vast cloud of witnesses" [1] spanning fifteen hundred years of people searching for God and being inspired to record their experiences and beliefs,

Setting the Scene

which change over time as we might expect. This is an ongoing story of which we need to be a part. It is a very human book which God adopts and uses.

We consider how much ideas change over time and why we should still read the Old Testament.

Lastly, we consider the important issue of how we teach the bible and present Christianity to the next generation and the world – the vital necessity of removing the image of God as a capricious tyrant.

Jesus: Our lens on the world

The Old Testament needs to be read through the lens of Jesus. In Jesus, God chose to live a real human life, suffering hardship, hunger, disappointment, frustration, insult, sorrow and betrayal. He died a humiliating and excruciatingly painful death on the cross, so that everyone could be rescued from sin and separation from God through his self-sacrificing love. Jesus' miracles gave life and health. He gave new life and hope to sinners and outcasts. He transformed the lives of those who had "ears to hear". He loved his enemies, as he taught others to do. He was passionate about condemning injustice and hypocrisy and was very forceful in criticising and challenging wrong actions and motives. Jesus warned of the damage people would do to their true selves by constant bad behaviour, but he never physically harmed anyone. He preached forgiveness. He forgave those who crucified him.[2] Even in his agony on the cross, he thought of his mother[3] and the penitent thief.[4] His whole life was one of self-giving love, service and compassion.

Human minds and hearts can never fully understand and know what God is like, but Christians believe that in Jesus we come closest to that knowledge. Jesus is the key to our understanding of God. He is the example, the yardstick with which to measure other events and attitudes, and the truth of what is said about God in other contexts, including other parts of the bible. *For Christians, Jesus must be the lens through which we look at the world and its problems and the troubling issues in the bible.*

Notes:

1. Heb. 12:1
2. Lk. 23:34
3. Jn. 19:26
4. Lk. 23:43

Part One

The Problem

1. The Bible is a Very Human Book

Magazines often carry a disclaimer: "The views expressed in this publication are not necessarily those of the editor." I think it would be a good idea if every bible came with a similar disclaimer: "The views expressed in this book are not necessarily those of God." A great deal of misunderstanding would be avoided.

The bible is a very human book but God has adopted it. He did not write it but he has accepted it as the record of his people's search for him and their attempts, sometimes making mistakes, to understand him. God uses this bible, despite all its faults, as a vehicle for communication, to guide and inspire those who wish to be his children.

Most people love their children but that does not mean that they like everything they do or agree with everything they say. Hopefully, parents do their best to encourage, support and guide them as much as is possible. I'm sure that God does not agree with every statement made in the bible or endorse every action that its characters take. The many violent acts attributed to God in the Old Testament certainly come into this category. The bible expresses so many contrasting and contradictory views that they cannot all be correct; they cannot all be God's opinion. The bible speaks with a disjointed chorus of human voices. That does not prevent it from being a unique source of inspiration which God can use to speak to those who have hearts and ears to listen and hear. God uses imperfect people and he can use an imperfect bible.

Regardless of its imperfections, this amazing collection of writings which we have come to know as, "The bible" has inspired people of many ages, races and cultures over the centuries, and continues to do so. Millions have heard God speaking to them through its pages, and come to know

God in their lives. It brings us the inestimable love of God in the Good News of Jesus Christ. Its value and importance cannot be over-emphasised. Like people, the bible is more than the sum of its parts because God has adopted it.

Despite this, it is also true that many people are put off the bible and therefore put off Christianity by some troubling aspects of the bible. One major problem is the violent image of God portrayed in large sections of the Old Testament. Christians must reject this image and focus on Jesus.

2. The Violent Acts of God

There are hundreds of instances where God orders, approves, or himself carries out acts of extreme violence. They are disturbing. They are shocking. They are immoral. They need to be recognised as such. They are also an integral part of the Old Testament saga and cannot be ignored but they should never be accepted as true representations of God.

We now look at some examples. Some may be well known, others perhaps not.

God orders genocide: The Book of Joshua

Imagine you have just turned to a news channel on your TV: "Breaking News: Joshua indicted for war crimes... accused of genocide... in defence, he says, 'I was just following orders... God told me to do it'."

In 2009 the International Criminal Court charged Omar al-Bashir, president of Sudan, with genocide, war crimes and crimes against humanity, for his actions against ethnic groups in Darfur.

The massacres described in the book of Joshua are just as bad. They should have the same outright condemnation.

The book of Joshua tells the story of the Israelites' invasion and conquest of Canaan, the "promised land", a land "flowing with milk and honey and people".[1] The people; men, women, children and initially also all the animals, were all to be slaughtered. If we take this text at face value, this was God's instruction to Moses now passed on to Joshua. "As for the towns that the Lord your God is giving you as an inheritance, you must not let anything that breathes remain alive. You shall annihilate them." (Deut.

20:16-17)

We all know the story of Jericho when the walls came tumbling down. The song and the children's story end at that point but continue reading in chapter six and there is a horrific blood bath.

According to the text, Joshua is doing exactly what God wishes. The complete annihilation of every person is repeated in the city of Ai and a whole list of thirty-one other towns.[2] An appalling picture of wholesale murder.

> "All the spoil of these towns and the livestock the Israelites took for their booty but all the people they struck down with the edge of the sword until they had destroyed them and they did not leave any who breathed... as the Lord had commanded his servant Moses." (Josh. 11:14-15)

On one occasion, just to be sure the destruction is complete, God rains down massive hail stones on those who are running away.[3] We are told that more people died from the hailstones than the Israelites killed with the sword.

A further disturbing addition to the Jericho story is that of Achan.[4] He is found to have disobeyed the instructions and stolen some valuable items from the city. Because God has been disobeyed, the Israelites are initially defeated by the residents of Ai. God has withdrawn his support. Achan is identified by casting lots and he and all his family are stoned to death. "Justice" has now been done and the Israelites can continue the successful massacres with God's renewed support.

Over the last century, a great deal of research has brought to light evidence from outside the bible which sheds light on these events and helps us to see them in the context of their time and culture. Documents from other ancient Near Eastern countries in the same period show more about what life was like. Life was short and hard and could be harsh and cruel. City-states had their own kings and regularly attacked one another in skirmishes over land. All believed in their own warrior gods who would be on their side and victory in war was seen as a victory and an honour to that god. The Israelites were doing the same as their neighbours in imagining their God as a warrior who would fight on their behalf.

It was also usual to greatly exaggerate the achievements to praise and honour the leader and the god. It is reasonable to suppose that Israelite stories were told in a similar way. They were part of a place and culture in time. That was how things worked.

Everything looks different when we look at it in context and this is just as true for the bible. This does not make the violence morally right but it does show that the Israelites were doing nothing unusual in thinking that conquest and slaughter were part of God's Plan. There are many passages within the bible to suggest that the people were not always sure that theirs was the only God. Perhaps he was just the best of the bunch.

The land of Canaan was a sought-after region, part of the "fertile crescent" and on important trade routes, which had constantly been fought over. In the fluctuations of power, it was most probably common practice to kill or enslave one's defeated enemies. The ten commandments say nothing about loving your enemy.

So that was what the Israelites believed. Do we have to believe that they were right? Do we have to believe that those instructions really came from the God we see in Jesus? I would say most definitely not. It is incredible even to consider the possibility that God ordered genocide. Perhaps the Israelites really thought that was true at the time but looking back through the Jesus lens, we have to say they got it wrong.

It is easy to see how such a policy could have been considered expedient. The Israelites wanted to keep their race pure and remain faithful to their God. The Golden Calf incident[5] (described below) had already shown how easily they could be influenced by the other cultures around them, and slide into the worship of other gods. To deduce that killing your enemies was not God's way would have been a considerable ethical and cultural leap at that time. It was not thought good policy to allow intermarriage or the worship of other gods to go on around them. They sought to remove the temptations and the risk of contamination.

It is not right and never was right, for one nation to be enslaved by another, so we can believe it to be in the nature of God to inspire leaders to do something about the situation, making use of the opportunities provided in the natural course of events. As refugees looking for a land they could call home, they needed a strong sense of identity and purpose, which being God's chosen people gave them. Wandering through the wilderness, they needed the structure and direction that Moses' laws provided. Having come from the harsh, restricted, and probably highly organised life of slavery, the absolute rules with predictable punishments were, to an extent, appropriate at that time to keep them together, focused on God, and with something to hope for at the end of the journey. All a very human process.

So, taking into account the overall conditions and prevailing culture of the time, we can see that the Israelites might have behaved in the ways described in the books of Exodus, Numbers, Deuteronomy and Joshua but that does not mean that God approved of or ordered the actions. The vast majority of people today would not hesitate to condemn the atrocities that have taken place in Rwanda, Cambodia, Serbia, Darfur, Syria and Ukraine, so why should we view the Canaan massacres differently because they are in the bible?

We need to condemn the Israelites' actions and recognise them as clearly incompatible with the character of God that we see in Jesus.

Did it actually happen at all?

So far we have criticised the conquest as it is presented in the book of Joshua but there is another very significant factor.

Further research and discovery, including extensive archaeological explorations, actually suggest that this massive conquest of the land probably never happened at all. It was probably a long and complex process of gradual settlement over many years. The bible itself gives contradictory evidence on this matter. In Joshua 10:40 we read:

> "So Joshua defeated the whole land, the hill country and the Negeb and the lowland slopes and all their kings; he left no one remaining, but utterly destroyed all that breathed, as the Lord God of Israel had commanded. And Joshua defeated them from Kadesh-barnea to Gaza and all the country of Goshen, as far as Gibeon. Joshua took all these kings

and their land at one time because the Lord God of Israel fought for Israel."

However, in the first chapter of the book of Judges, which continues the story, we are told that the people were still fighting the Canaanites and there were many towns where they had not all been driven out.

That might seem to let God off the hook to a certain extent but it is still vital to say we do not believe that God was responsible for sanctioning violence against women and children and non-combatants, whatever the level involved. Even if these events never happened at all, the fact remains that the bible says they did and that still needs to be challenged. The stories are mainly read and told as though they *did* actually happen and were ordered and approved by God. The question mark over their historical accuracy is not mentioned. Without the external evidence, we should still be prepared to say that it must not be true that God ordered genocide.

We move away from Jericho and the invasion of Canaan, to consider other examples of God's violence.

The Golden Calf. (Exod. 32): God's double punishment
This incident is another example of how God's so-called actions in the Old Testament contrast heavily with the actions of Jesus. According to this story, God orders the mass murder of his own people, the Israelites, as punishment for the sin of the community and also inflicts devastating illness.

This story takes place before the conquest of Canaan. The Israelites are camped in the desert after escaping from slavery in Egypt. Moses has gone up the mountain to receive the ten commandments and the people become restless because he has been gone a long time. They want a visual symbol and ask Aaron to "make them gods to lead us." He collects their gold earrings and fashions an image of a golden calf which the people worship. They have broken the second commandment, "You shall not make for yourself an idol in the form of anything... you shall not bow down to them or worship them."[6] The bull was a common symbol of a god in Canaanite culture.

God is angry and threatens to destroy them all but Moses pleads on the people's behalf and God changes his mind but severe punishment is to follow. The Levites gather to Moses and he instructs them;

> "Thus says the Lord the God of Israel, 'Put your sword on your side. Go... throughout the camp and each of you kill your brother, your friend and your neighbour' and about 3,000 of the people fell on that day."[7]

Not content with this punishment, God then sent a plague on the people because they had made the calf. This is how the Old Testament frequently interprets the character of God. His judgements are harsh and destructive and often involve inflicting illness and death on a large scale.

In sharp contrast, Jesus healed

Jesus healed hundreds of people with all kinds of diseases and disabilities. When a woman touched his cloak, believing that she could be healed, Jesus "felt power go out of him."[8] It was not something that took no effort. Yet we have snapshots in the gospels which show how people flocked to him for healing and can imagine how this went on all the time wherever he went.

> "Now when the sun was setting, all those who had any who were sick with various kinds of diseases

brought them to him; and he laid his hands on each of them and cured them." (Luke 4:41-42)

Mark tells us it was difficult to find time to eat.[9] Jesus had to escape to lonely places to pray and recharge his batteries.

When John the Baptist's followers ask about Jesus, they are told, "Go and tell John what you have seen and heard: the blind receive their sight, the lame walk, the lepers are cleansed, the deaf hear, the dead are raised..."[10]

Can we really imagine Jesus reversing this healing process and deliberately inflicting illness on anyone? It is Jesus who shows us the real character of God, bringing renewed life, hope and health, not the harsh reprisals of the golden calf incident.

There are other areas of life where Jesus takes a very different stance from that of the rigid Old Testament laws. A notable example is their respective approaches to the Sabbath Day customs which can be seen in the following story.

A savage Old Testament Sabbath

Sabbath Day observance was very important throughout bible times but we see a clear distinction in the attitude to the Sabbath Day rules between the Old Testament and Jesus.

According to the first creation story in Genesis, "God finished the work that he had done, and he rested on the seventh day from all the work that he had done. So God blessed the seventh day and hallowed it."[11]

The fourth of the ten commandments says that because of this no work must be done on the Sabbath day.[12] Detailed rules evolved to determine exactly what could or could not be done on the Sabbath and the Israelites were keen on keeping to them. It could, of course, be seen as a good and enlightened policy that gave people a day's rest from work and one in which slaves and animals were specifically included. But the penalty for disobedience was death.[13]

When the Israelites were living in the wilderness, they found a man gathering sticks on the Sabbath day. They brought him to Moses and he was taken into custody because it was not clear what should be done to him. This seems to suggest that the death penalty was not always applied. "Then the Lord said to Moses, the man shall be put to death; all the congregation shall stone him outside the camp"[14] and this is what happened.

In contrast: a Gospel Sabbath with Jesus.

By the time we get to the New Testament, it is obvious that the Sabbath day was still strictly adhered to. It is one of the main sources of conflict between the religious authorities and Jesus, although the death penalty is no longer mentioned. There is no reason to believe that Jesus did not keep the Sabbath day in general. Luke tells us that Jesus went to the synagogue on the Sabbath "as was his custom."[15] However, Jesus saw caring for people in need as being more important than keeping to the letter of the law.

There are several specific stories of healing on the Sabbath and the controversy this causes. Jesus heals a blind man, a man with a withered hand, an epileptic, a woman who was disfigured and unable to stand straight, and the man who had sat by the pool of Bethesda for thirty-eight years hoping for a cure.[16] In response to his critics, Jesus asks, "Is it lawful to do good or to do harm on the Sabbath, to save life or to kill?"[17] He points out the inconsistencies of some of the things that *were* allowed. "The Sabbath was made for humankind, not humankind for the Sabbath,"[18] sums up the way Jesus modified the commandment to fulfil the spirit and intention of the law rather than the legalistic interpretation followed by many of the religious leaders. Jesus risked his own safety by antagonising the religious leaders in this way. He obviously thought it important. We are told that Jesus' disciples plucked ears of grain to eat as they walked through a corn field on the Sabbath.[19] Jesus was with them and defended their actions.

Given all these incidents, we certainly cannot imagine Jesus condemning a man to be stoned to death for collecting a few sticks on the Sabbath.

Swallowed up

There are many other violent and disturbing events described as the Israelites wander for forty years through the wilderness. As may seem realistic, there was much tension and dissatisfaction in the camps as our next story, which also takes place during this time, illustrates. God is described as being ruthless in dealing with troublemakers. They are "swallowed up" into the earth.

In this story, God acts directly to zap the offending individuals. A group rebels against Moses and Aaron, grumbling about the way things are organised and perhaps wanting more power for themselves. Moses asks for a sign that it is still God's will for him to lead. In response to this request, the ground under the rebels and their families is split apart. "The earth opened its mouth and swallowed them up, along with their households... the earth closed over them."[20] The stuff of nightmares! "Fire came out from the Lord and consumed the 250 men" who had supported the protest.[21] Soon afterwards, another large number of people complain about what has happened. Again God proposes to destroy everyone and start again with Moses (as with Noah?). Again Moses intercedes on behalf of the people and God relents but severe punishment follows. Fourteen thousand seven hundred people are killed by a plague.[22]

The point of the story is to stress the divinely appointed leadership of Moses, so the punishment is attributed to God. The political strategy of disposing of dissidents is sadly still very observable in our world in the twenty-first century and was no doubt common in the ancient Near East. Those who dare to criticise are "swallowed up." They disappear.

Plagues which swept through populations would have been also very much a part of life. With the world as it was then, it does not take much imagination to say that we can now, with our more advanced knowledge, safely take God out of the picture in this respect. However, the writers of the Old Testament never took God out of the picture, so it may be useful at this point to think about the way they viewed their world.

An Israelite view of God and their world

Today's western culture tends to separate God out from most of what goes on in the world, but the Old Testament Israelites believed that God was directly responsible for everything that happened. There was for them no such things as science or the forces of nature. Everything that happened was decreed by God and was in response to people's behaviour, or some particular purpose of God. If the harvest was good, it was God's blessing. If the crops failed, it was a sign of God's displeasure. If an infestation of frogs came out of the river, God was responsible for putting them there. Plagues and what we would call natural disasters were seen as punishments for sin. This was the outlook from which they saw the world and this was the viewpoint from which they wrote their history. For them, a flood really was an "act of God". They attributed violent acts to God, which the God shown in Jesus could never have perpetrated.

The stories were written to declare God's victory and power over all creation, human empires and all their gods. Also, they affirm the election and protection of Israel as the chosen people. It is God who fights on their behalf and deserves the glory. This was the ancient Israelites' way of seeing God and the world. We should see that God does not control events in this way today and believe that he did not do so then.

So what did happen?

It is possible to view all these stories of God's destructive acts in different ways. We can look at them in the context of the ancient Near East and its belief systems and say that all these actions and events could have happened (perhaps with some exaggeration) through natural or human actions and that they could have been mistakenly attributed to God.

We can also see the stories as having some root in history but having been retold and reshaped through the centuries before being recorded in their final form to serve a particular theological or political purpose.

Some people would say that it all actually happened just as the bible says. I believe this to be incompatible with the nature of God as shown in Jesus and an unrealistic interpretation of the situation. It should be unthinkable that God could ever have behaved like an angry, vindictive, cruel, unforgiving and unpredictable human.

I regret that there are yet more Old Testament horror stories that need to be identified because it is important to see just how extensive the problem is. We are not looking at just a few untypical incidents. Our next story moves into yet another dimension. A whole nation is to be permanently cursed for what their ancestors did two hundred years earlier!

Those cursed Amalekites!

This is a story of another harsh judgement from God which happens at a much later period in time when Israel has a king.[23]

The prophet Samuel brings a message from God to King Saul:

> "Thus says the lord of hosts, 'I will punish the Amalekites for what they did in opposing the Israelites when they came up out of Egypt. Now go and attack the Amalekites and utterly destroy all that they have; do not spare them but kill both man and woman, child and infant, ox and sheep, camel and donkey." (1 Samuel 15:1-3)

Saul obediently gathers a large army and marches to the Amalekites' city. People of other tribes are allowed to leave before the Israelites attack. The Amalekites are all duly killed as God supposedly ordered. However, Agag, the king of the Amalekites, is taken alive and the people keep the best of the animals. God then tells Samuel that he is very angry with Saul for not carrying out his instructions to the full. Samuel passes this on to Saul in very forceful language, saying that God has rejected him as king because of his disobedience. Saul repents and asks forgiveness (for not killing the king). Samuel summons King Agag and "hews him in pieces before the Lord" in a ritual execution. God does not change his mind. The Amalekites are to be blotted out and Saul is rejected as king of Israel. Saul, it seems, was more merciful than God or the prophet. This is a curse from God that lasts for generations.

This is rather like suggesting that we should kill every German alive now because of what the Nazis did eighty years ago! The biblical time gap was longer, about 200 years.

We can see how this action and belief system might fit into the ancient Near Eastern culture and practice but there is no way we can say that it portrays the God we see in Jesus.

We have now read various examples, from different time periods within the Old Testament illustrating the violent, punitive and destructive acts of God, but does any of it compare in numbers and horror with what is about to follow?

Saving the worst until last: The Flood. (Genesis 6-8)

We have looked at some shocking illustrations but God's greatest destructive act tends to be glossed over. This is the story of the Flood. God sees the wickedness of human beings. He is sorry he made the world and decides to destroy it. He decides to destroy everything he has created: all the people, all the animals, everything that grows. Only Noah and his family and specimens of all the creatures are to be saved. Every other living thing on the earth is gradually drowned as the waters rise over the world. Creation is a disappointment, a failed experiment. Everything is blotted out.

No doubt there were many disastrous floods in the ancient Near East. We have seen the devastation caused by floods and tsunamis in our own time. Before the existence of modern communication systems and international aid agencies, it may have felt as though the whole world was involved. There are about three hundred similar disaster stories told throughout the ancient world. They are usually said to be the action of the gods. A story from the ancient Near East has many facts in common with the biblical account and is much older. It is part of a Babylonian story called *The Epic of Gilgamesh*. However, the bible story has important differences to give it theological significance. God decides on the flood because the people are wicked. Only Noah and his family and specimens of all the creatures are to be saved. God then makes a new covenant or agreement with Noah. There are other instances in the story of Moses where God threatens to destroy the Israelites when they have been disobedient, such as the making of a golden calf and rebellion against Moses (both previously described) but God is persuaded to change his mind. Was this something the Israelites feared might happen? The theme of God's judgement and rescue is repeated in many ways and circumstances throughout the Old Testament.

Most of the flood story focuses on Noah and his ark. Little space is given to the victims: the rest of the population and all the creatures who were to be "blotted out from the earth". Are we to believe that every child was wicked? Were the animals wicked? Think realistically about what is happening. We've all seen news reports from recent disasters; women sitting precariously on rooftops clutching small children or crowds gathered on hilltops hoping to be rescued. In the days of Genesis, there were no helicopters as the waters rose higher than the mountains. Imagine the scene of panic and despair in the worst disaster movie! To regard this as a factual story about the loving God we see in Jesus is nothing less than character assassination. If we accept the nature of God as shown in the teaching and actions of Jesus, how is it possible to believe that a few centuries earlier his policy had been to wipe everyone out in a very cruel way and start again? No, the message of the cross is that God will not give up and dispose of us – despite the mess we make of his plans. Jesus was always God's plan. He does not change his mind.

It can be argued that God was entitled to destroy the world as a failed experiment. It might even have been fair. But the God Christians believe in goes way beyond fair. He is supremely generous. He offers us forgiveness. He offers us life, now and forever; not death and destruction:

> "For God so loved the world that he gave his only Son, so that everyone who believes in him may not perish but may have eternal life. Indeed, God did not send the Son into the world to condemn the world, but in order that the world might be saved through him." (John 3:16-17)

In his article on Genesis in the Oxford bible Commentary, R.N. Whybray writes:

> "Stories of a great flood sent in primaeval times to destroy mankind are so common to many peoples in different parts of the world between whom no kind of historical contact seems possible that the theme seems almost to be a universal feature of the human imagination. The flood story in Genesis is a clear example of a type that was characteristic of the Mesopotamian world."

On a positive note, the flood story gives us the legend of the origin of the rainbow. Nowadays, having a scientific explanation for this does not at all reduce the sense of beauty and wonder or the feeling of hope and encouragement the sight of a rainbow in the sky can inspire.

Notes

1. Ex 3:8
Also Prior: 98
2. Josh 12
3. Josh 10:11
4. Josh 7
5. Ex 32
6. Ex 20:4-5
7. Ex 32:27-28
8. Mk. 5:30
9. Mk 3:20
10. Lk 7:22
11. Gen 2:2-3
12. Ex 20:8-11
13. Ex 31:14
14. Num. 15:32-36
15. Lk 4:16
16. Jn 5:2-9
17. Mk 3:4
18. Mk 2:27
19. Lk 6:1
20. Num 16:31
21. Num 16:35
22. Num 16:49
23. 1 Sam 15

3. "Virtuous Violence"
Don't Count the Dead

If all the gruesome accounts of battles are taken as true, they did count the dead. It was a badge of honour. "Saul has killed his thousands, and David his tens of thousands."[1]

Authors and filmmakers write in such a way as to suggest how we should feel about their characters and events. "The cavalry charged, the Indians died. You don't count the dead when God's on your side" says a 1960s protest song.[2] Western films with cowboys and Indians used to be very popular; there were not many that featured "good" Indians. You were supposed to cheer when the bugle sounded and the cavalry appeared over the hill. Never mind that the white invaders had stolen the Indian's land and sacred places. They were the "good guys."

When reading about the conquest of "The Promised Land" we are conditioned to be on the side of the Israelites – conditioned by years of tradition, Sunday school lessons, sermons and commentaries. "It's in the bible and it says God ordered it, so it must be true and it must be OK," seems to have been the generally accepted thought. To see it objectively, we have to read *against the grain*. Imagine the situation from the point of view of the frightened people inside the walls of Jericho. How might they have told the story? How is it that people can readily accept atrocities in the bible, which in any other context would be condemned out of hand? The Israelites were the aggressors. They invaded another nation's territories and took them by force. They showed no mercy to the inhabitants. They slaughtered whole populations – non-combatants, women, children and animals.

We now have the New Testament. We have the example of the life and death of Jesus as witness to the love of God for all people. How can we possibly believe that the same God ever ordered or wanted such horrific acts?

Violence constitutes a major part of so many of the best-known Old Testament stories. It is frequently portrayed as a good thing. In his book *The Violence of Scripture,* Eric Seibert uses the phrase "virtuous violence"[3] to describe this. The violent acts that instinct should tell us to condemn, are portrayed as good and even praised and rewarded by God. This is how the incidents are presented. Murder and treachery become "virtuous" actions. This is what the text asks us to think. Take all these stories away from association with God and the bible and they would be evaluated very differently. The conquest triumphs of Israel such as the battle of Jericho are an obvious example. There are many more both collective and individual.

Experiments have been done which illustrate this. A group of children aged eight to fourteen were asked their opinion of a genocidal passage in Joshua. Sixty-six per cent said they approved the action. Another similar group were given an account supposedly relating to the actions of an ancient Chinese general and only seven per cent said they approved.[4] We need to read with our brains and critical faculties in gear. We need to read with imaginative compassion. We need to see the rape, murder, vengeance and genocide for what they are: despicable actions which would never be sanctioned by the loving God we see in Jesus. Of course, many nations, tribes and individuals behaved in these ways and still do but that is a very different thing from claiming that they are of God.

What follows is a glaring example of this supposedly virtuous violence.

The story of Phinehas: hero or murderer?
This is another gruesome story which would merit an 18+ certificate. The gory details are in Numbers 25. This also happens during the forty years of wandering in the wilderness between leaving Egypt and entering the Promised Land. Israelite men began to have sexual relations with women of Moab. This led them into the worship of other gods worshipped by the Moabites. Both these things were against the law of God and he gets angry. Following God's orders, Moses orders all who have entered into these relationships to be killed. An Israelite then arrived with a foreign woman and took her into his family tent. Then Phinehas, the son of Moses' brother Aaron, followed them and "pierced the two of them through the belly" with a spear. God praised Phinehas for having "such zeal on my behalf." And rewards him, "I hereby grant him my covenant of peace. It shall be for him and for his descendants after him a covenant of perpetual priesthood, because he was zealous for his God, and made atonement for the Israelites." His violent act is meant to be seen as virtuous and he is praised and handsomely rewarded!

Our next example of "virtuous violence", like the flood, is a very well-known story which seems to be generally accepted without question. The Israelites were saved, the baddies died and God was triumphant!

The sea red with blood
Exodus 14 describes crossing the Red Sea and drowning the Egyptian army. It even says that God deliberately planned it this way so that he would, "Gain glory for myself over Pharaoh and all his army and his chariots and his chariot drivers; and the Egyptians shall know that I am

the Lord." [5] He "hardened Pharaoh's heart" so that he changed his mind about letting the Israelites go and decided to pursue them. It's a brilliant, dramatically told, emotional story. The enslaved underdogs win. It's a great result. (Except for the ordinary Egyptian soldiers and their families.) It has captured the filmmakers' hearts. It has been made into blockbuster films that hugely influence people's imaginations and impressions of the event.

It also forms part of the ancient Easter liturgy and is part of the defining story of Jewish faith.

BUT. And it is a very large BUT. That is not the way God behaves. He does not lure people into doing bad things. He does not seek self-aggrandisement by harming others. If we choose to believe in the miracle of rolling back the sea, the water could simply have been returned between the Israelites and the army and no one would have been killed. If God can do anything, why not just put up a forcefield? They did not have to all drown. Moving to the bigger picture, Marcus Borg writes:

> "... the issue is whether God has ever acted anywhere, any time, as portrayed in the plagues of Egypt and the crossing of the sea. To say that God did so act in Moses' day is to leave inexplicable the non-interventions in situations of intense human suffering in the centuries ever since." [6]

There are many obvious examples. The Holocaust happened. At the time of writing, the Russian army under Putin is ruthlessly devastating Ukraine and killing its civilians. God does not go around zapping the bullies in spectacular and unmistakable ways. Jesus was clearly against injustice and oppression but the most violent thing he is recorded as doing is his demonstration against the Temple systems which allowed traders and the Temple authorities to exploit worshippers but he never physically harmed anyone. Jesus shows us that God cares about and shares our human condition but not by copying humans in responding with violence.

God cares

There are other ways in which to "see" the whole Exodus story. Again, as in the conquest of Canaan, we have to ask, "Did it actually happen?" Most researchers agree that it is not historically accurate. It probably has some basis in actual events and grew over time through a mixture of memory and imagination and passed on tradition.

The exodus story is a very powerful one which resonates with people living in, or escaping from, situations of oppression. It affirms that God cares about their plight. It says that God is right there alongside them. It says that God wants people to be rescued from slavery, abuse, torture and any kind of oppressive domination. It says that God will inspire and strengthen those who work and campaign for the freedom, fair treatment, equality and social justice of others. This is a message that is true for all people in all times and places. It can do this as "story" without insisting on it being literally true in all details, which would distort the character of God. Taken literally, God was a war criminal. We will explore more about the power of "story" in a later chapter. Jesus identified with the oppressed and made promises. The persecuted will be first in the kingdom of heaven. All tyrannical powers will fail and fall in the end; no dictator or oppressive regime lasts forever. God works in ways undetectable to those who do not wish to believe. He does not act in spectacular ways which are obvious to everyone; the risen Jesus did not make a dramatic appearance in the Temple or walk through Jerusalem. His kingdom will last forever. Ultimately, good *will* overcome evil.

Notes

1. 1 Sam 18:7
2. Bob Dylan, 1963 *With God on our side* Warner Bros.
3. Seibert (2012, p.27)
4. Jenkins (2012, p185)
5. Ex 14:17-18
6. Borg (1989, p103)

4. Sexism and Discrimination

Another aspect of life, where a very significant difference in attitude between parts of the Old Testament and Jesus can be seen, is in the treatment of people who were generally devalued, marginalised and excluded by society and the customs of the time. Much of this was based on laws which were deemed to come from God and still applied in Jesus' time. Jesus spent time with women and children, the despised tax collectors, prostitutes, people with infectious diseases, people with disabilities and anyone in need. He cared for them all and assured them that they were of value to God, who longed for them to choose to be a part of his heavenly kingdom. It is surely Jesus' attitude that shows us the true nature of God.

Women in the Old Testament are very much second-class citizens. Remembering that the bible is a very human book, this is not surprising as that was mostly the situation in the world at the time and has been in the majority of history ever since. In the ancient Near East, women were subordinate to men and this was not questioned. It was simply how things were. That does not mean that it was how things should be or that it was what God intended. It was a patriarchal society in which a woman was the property of her father and then her husband. She did all the hard work but had no voice. The image of "a perfect wife" in Proverbs 31 says it all! It is praising her value as a servant to her husband and family, not as a person. The other proverbs concerning women are mainly derogatory and all from a male perspective. Men could have more than one wife and could divorce a wife just because "she did not please him."[1]

Exodus 22:16 says, "When a man seduces a virgin who is not engaged to be married and lies with her, he shall give the bride price for her and make her his wife. But if her father refuses to give her to him, he shall pay an amount equal to the bride-price for virgins." A man could sell his daughter as a slave to another Israelite and she would not be released after seven years as would a male slave.[2] There are rules controlling her further treatment which at the time would be considered enlightened compared with other cultures around but she still had no say in the matter. It was all up to the men. The punishment for adultery if caught in the act was officially death for both the man and the woman. However, a wife accused of adultery had to go through an extremely unpleasant and elaborate ritual before a priest, which supposedly determined her guilt or innocence but there is no mention of the man concerned.[3] These rules are supposedly given by God to Moses. There are instances of women raped by outsiders who are savagely avenged but it seems more a matter of family honour than concern for the women. When a woman is abused, the compensation is because the father or husband has been dishonoured. His property has been spoiled. The tenth commandment lists your neighbour's wife as something you must not covet, along with other property!

Women were expendable
In a horrific incident described in Judges (beginning in chapter 19:22), a man is entertaining a guest at his home when some drunken gang demand the guest come out so that they can, "have intercourse with him." The householder offers his virgin daughter and concubine instead, saying they could treat them as they wish. "Only don't do such a vile thing to my guest!" The same situation occurs in Genesis 19 when Lot says, "Look, I have two daughters who have not known a man; let me bring them

out to you and do to them as you please; only do nothing to these men, for they have come under the shelter of my roof." Hospitality was a duty and honour and was more important than the treatment or life of a mere woman. That is how it was.

Women were brutally slaughtered in battles and were routinely taken as spoils of war and then blamed for leading Israelite men to worship their gods. Women were abducted to provide wives when there was a shortage of Israelite women.[4]

A woman was "unclean" after childbirth and during menstruation.[5] Her bed and anything she sat on and anyone who touched those things was unclean for the rest of the day. The purification time following a birth was double if the child was a girl. This custom continues into the time of Jesus. Mary and Joseph take Jesus to the temple, "When the time came for their purification according to the law of Moses."[6] The woman with the haemorrhage who was healed when she touched Jesus' cloak, had been unclean for twelve years and would have been a social outcast as a result and afraid to be found in such a crowd.[7]

Can we really believe that this attitude to women was what God ever intended and ordered?

The attitude shown by Jesus

Jesus had women followers. We can tell from the Martha and Mary story that they were not just there to provide food, etc. Mary is encouraged to listen and learn from Jesus.[8] On several occasions, he had conversations with women such as the Samaritan woman at the well. It was clearly unusual in that culture because the disciples were surprised.[9]

Jesus does not condemn the woman to death who was caught in adultery and cleverly diverts her accusers. He does not condone the act, she is to, "go and sin no more."[10] He understands and is sympathetic to the woman who anoints his head with expensive ointment [11] and the one who washes his feet with her tears.[12] He always had time for the rejected and marginalised which included many women. Prostitution was about the only occupation open to a woman with no male support. Otherwise, she would be dependent on charity. Jesus praised the faith of the woman who touched his cloak believing that she would be healed.[13] When he restores the widow of Nain's son back to life the emphasis is on the widow. Without her only son, she had no support.[14]

Luke tells the birth stories from Mary's point of view[15] and according to John, Mary Magdalene is the first person to see the risen Christ.[16]

Does the position of women improve in the Early New Testament Church?

Compared with that of the Old Testament, the position of women does seem to have begun to improve in the early New Testament church, probably as a result of Jesus' attitude.

The Acts of the Apostles and some of the later letters show differing views of the position of women. The letter to Timothy, an epistle written towards the end of the New Testament period, is the most controlling. "Let a woman learn in silence with full submission. I permit no woman to teach or to have authority over a man." [17] This text is still used by those who reject the ordination of women.

In the Acts of the Apostles, we are told about women who became active believers. Lydia, a dealer in purple cloth, was seemingly able to carry out a trade.[18] Paul refers to *Lydia's* home and *her* household.[19] There were "leading women" in Thessalonica.[20] Paul travelled with Aquilla *and Priscilla*, refugees from Rome, who like him were tentmakers.[21]

Tabitha, in Joppa, is described as a disciple[22]

In his letters to the Christian communities, Paul sends greetings to, "sister Phoebe, a deacon"[23] as well as several other women. In Romans 16:7, Junia is described as an apostle. Paul refers to *Chloe's* people.[24] Women appear to have been leaders of house churches.

The Old Testament characters Rahab and Ruth appear in Matthew's genealogy of Christ.[25]

Sadly, the church in later years seems to have moved backwards and been more influenced by texts that subordinate women, such as Ephesians 5:22-24. It does tell husbands to love their wives as themselves but, "Wives be subject to your husbands as you are to the Lord. For the husband is the head of the wife... just as the church is subject to Christ, so also wives ought to be, in everything to their husbands." Here are rules written by men for the benefit of men, reflecting the accepted culture of the time. That does not mean that it was God's view or that it should have any bearing on life today. But around the world, this text and others still restrict and rule the lives of countless women.

A British woman, whose husband had recently retired, told me that she had lost her freedom. Although she had been efficiently running their house for forty years, they now organised things the way her husband chose because he was the man and the bible says that the man is the head of the woman. This, in the twenty-first century!

A very male God?

God is not male.

However, God has always been traditionally referred to (and probably mainly thought of) as male. In recent years some people, (men as well as women) considering this misleading and wishing to redress the balance, have begun to call God, "she". God is not a human being. God does not have a physical body. God is not male or female. God does not have any gender. God exists in an entirely different way to human beings. We do not have a polite neutral pronoun in English – "it" normally only referring to inanimate objects and animals. This makes it difficult to speak of God without using "he" or "she". We traditionally think of God as Father but there is no reason not to equally think of God as mother. Calling God Father can be a very unhelpful image for people who have bad or negative experiences of human fathers.

There are instances where the bible talks of God using female metaphors. In Isaiah 49:15, God speaks to Israel: "Can a woman forget her nursing child, or show no compassion for the child of her womb? Even these may forget but I will not forget you." And, "As a mother comforts her child, so I will comfort you." (Is 66:13)

Jesus, lamenting over Jerusalem, said: "How often have I desired to gather your children together as a hen gathers her brood under her wings?" (Luke 13:34)

So we need to remember that in the New Testament 'father' is used as a metaphor, as are 'son', 'shepherd', 'rock', 'vine', 'bread of life', 'light of the world' and all the expressions which try to explain the wonder of God and of Jesus. They are there to help us understand the immensity and the closeness of God's love, care and guidance through recognisable, concrete, everyday features of the time. They are not meant to limit our imaginations to restricted static images of God.

Treatment of children.
In biblical times, families wanted sons to carry on the family line and women who could not have children were looked down upon. When Elizabeth conceives John the Baptist, she says, "The Lord... looked favourably on me and took away the disgrace I have endured among my people." [26]

No doubt children were cared for in their families but in society, they were low in status. Proverbs 23:13 says, "Do not withhold discipline from your children: if you beat them with a rod they will not die. If you beat them with a rod you will save their lives from Sheol."

Children are frequently slaughtered in war along with everyone else and some ancient Near Eastern countries practised child sacrifice. When Abraham thinks God wants him to sacrifice his son Isaac, he seems to see it as something that could possibly be required.[27]

In Judges 11, a tragic story is told. Jephthah makes a vow to God that if he is victorious in the oncoming battle, he will sacrifice whoever is the first person to come out of his house to greet him when he returns. It is his daughter, his only child, who comes out to meet him. Whom did he expect? It's difficult to think of a more stupid promise. Despite his distress, she is sacrificed. Keeping his vow is more important than his daughter's life. He believes that God will expect and require this, as does his daughter, who perhaps significantly, is never named.

Now we turn to the gospels to see Jesus' very different attitude to children. When people brought children to Jesus to be blessed, the disciples at first turned them away. "But when Jesus saw this he was indignant and said to them, 'Let the little children come to me; do not stop them, for it is to such as these that the kingdom of God belongs'... and he took them up in his arms, laid his hands on them and blessed them."[28] He is happy to walk to the house of Jairus to cure his sick daughter.[29] Another time Jesus tells his disciples, "Whoever receives one such child in my name receives me."[30] We have several instances of Jesus using children as illustrations in his teaching, such as his teaching about humility when some followers are arguing about their own importance.[31]

Disability
There are passages in the Old Testament which make disturbing reading for people with disabilities.

Only perfect animals could be offered for sacrifice and the same applied to those men who performed the ceremonies. Aaron and his descendants were to be the Levites who offered the sacrifices in the sanctuary but God's instructions are:

> "No one of your offspring throughout their generations who has a blemish may approach to offer the food of his God. For no one who has a blemish shall draw near, one who is blind or lame or one who has a mutilated face or a limb too long or one who has a broken foot or a broken hand or a hunchback or a dwarf or a man with a blemish in his eyes or an itching disease or scabs or crushed testicles... He shall not approach the altar ... that he shall not profane my sanctuaries: for I am the Lord."
> (Lev 21:16-23)

And:

> "No one whose testicles are crushed or whose penis is cut off shall be admitted to the assembly of the

Lord." (Deut 23:1)

In contrast, Jesus cured people with all manner of disabilities and famously "touched lepers."[32] The gospels record over twenty-five specific accounts of Jesus healing men, women and children suffering from a variety of physical and mental disorders as well as the accounts of crowds gathering for his healing touch. It was clearly a major part of his ministry.

His association with characters who were generally shunned by "respectable" society was also an important feature which marked him out as having very different priorities and values from the religious leaders of the time. Jesus' attitude updates the discriminatory laws of the Old Testament. If Jesus could discount them, so can we. Jesus shows us the true response of God. In his eyes, everyone was of value and no one was "unclean" or excluded.

Notes
1. Deut 24:1
2. Ex 21:7
3. Num 5:12-31
4. Jud. 21
5. Lev 15:19-30
6. Lk 2:22-24
7. Mt 9:20-22
8. Lk 10:38-42
9. Jn 4:7
10. Jn 8:3-11
11. Mk 14:3-9
12. Lk 7:37
13. Mt 9:20-22
14. Lk 7:11-17
15. Lk 1:26-56
16. Jn 20:14-18
17. 1 Tim 2:11-12
18. Acts 16:14
19. Acts 16
20. Acts 17
21. Acts 18
22. Acts 9:36
23. Rom. 16:1

Disowning the Violence

24. I Cor 1:11
25. Mt 1:5
26. Lk 1:24-25
27. Gen 22
28. Mk 10:13-16
29. Mk 5:22
30. Mk 9:37
31. Mt 18:1-4
32. Lk 5:13

5. Has the Bible Encouraged Violence?

Most things can be used for good or for bad – nuclear power, wealth, the press, the Internet, social media, fame, power and influence, church traditions and many more. We can certainly add the bible to this list.

Throughout history, human beings, including those who would call themselves Christians, have carried out horrific acts of violence and cruelty in the name of God. So-called holy wars, religious war and persecutions between Catholic and protestant, witch hunts, hundreds of so-called heretics burned at the stake, the Spanish inquisition, wholesale slaughter of indigenous populations by explorers and settlers, anti-Semitism, slavery, racism, mistreatment of women and children, religious intolerance and countless other acts of cruelty and oppression. All have claimed justification from the bible. Some explorers and settlers saw themselves as entering the "promised land." Indigenous people were labelled as evil in the way that the Canaanites or the Amalekites were called evil. Of course, people have always used religion as a convenient excuse for gaining power and oppressing and victimising those who are different or stand in their way. Monarchs, politicians, church leaders, explorers and colonisers and other figures of authority have all been guilty of this in countless situations. Some genuinely believed that they were carrying out the will of God. If the massacres and harsh punishments ordered by God in the Old Testament are taken at face value and believed to be literally true, they provide a good precedent for such an attitude! How much did the crusades and so-called holy wars take their example from here? The biblical claim to the "Promised Land" still fuels support for the State of Israel's persecution of the indigenous Palestinians.

The crusades involved appalling acts of mass cruelty on both sides. During the first crusade in 1099, Pope Gregory 7th quoted Jeremiah 48:10 when rallying his troops, "Accursed is the one who keeps back the sword from bloodshed." [1] Thousands of Muslims, Jews, and Arab Christians including women and children were slaughtered in Jerusalem in an attack reminiscent of Jericho.

A soldier wrote, "It was a just and splendid judgement of God, that this place should be filled with the blood of unbelievers when it had suffered so long from their blasphemies." [2]

Had they read the Gospels?

Oliver Cromwell justified the massacre of hundreds of Irish Catholics. He slaughtered the populations of Irish towns such as Wexford by calling them Midianites and Amalekites.[3]

In times when western countries were busy colonising other parts of the world, some saw their actions in terms of the Israelites being given the promised land. There are many instances of biblical stories and texts being used in support of colonial practices that devastated the indigenous inhabitants of those lands. The Mystic River massacre in 1637 was one such event.[4] Puritan settlers in New England burned a whole village of the Indian Pequot tribe, also killing those who tried to escape. They used the Old Testament scripture in Judges 20 to justify the atrocity. Spaniards described West Indians as contemporary versions of Canaanites.[5] Many excused their exploits by reference to God's curse on Noah's son's descendants or the order to destroy the Amalekites in perpetuity.[6] They viewed the inhabitants of these new lands in those terms.

In the American civil war, both sides appealed to the Old Testament to justify their position. Slave owners argued that slavery was right because it was so evident in the bible. They should at least have also taken notice of the texts that say slaves are not to be treated harshly.[7]

In 1994 the horrific Rwandan genocide saw 800,000 people of Tutsi and other minority ethnic groups murdered by the Hutu majority. Some pastors used biblical passages to encourage people to kill their neighbours.[8]

The story of Phinehas has been previously mentioned. An American group calling themselves Vigilantes of Christendom or the "Phinehas priesthood" advocate white supremacy and claim Old Testament precedent for terrorist racist attacks on mixed-race couples and abortion clinics. Down the centuries, Phinehas was frequently put forward as a role model to encourage slaughter, which supposedly carried out the will of God.

Some saw it as their duty to beat children because of Old Testament texts such as, "Those who spare the rod hate their children, but those who love them are diligent to discipline them."[9]

As already discussed in chapter five, the general treatment of women in much of the bible and the literal acceptance of its teaching about women's subordination to men and place in society has been, and for many still is, a massive negative influence.

With all the violence described in the bible, it is not difficult to find a text to "justify" things which someone actually wants to do for other reasons. Religion has rarely been the real or sole motive for all the atrocities committed but it played a part. It provided an excuse.

It is, therefore, vital that those who speak in Christ's name state clearly that the violence invoked in the bible does not represent the true nature or desire of God. For this, we must keep focusing on Jesus. He would never approve of acts of murder, oppression, injustice or any kind of cruelty. If this belief was officially expressed and generally accepted, it would reduce the plausibility of those who ridicule the bible because of the violent images of God or misuse it to justify harming others.

Notes
1. Seibert, 2012, p377
2. Seibert, 2012, p.363
3. Flood, 2014 p.202
4. Seibert, 2012 p.80
5. Enns, 1989 p.496
6. Gen. 9:20-27
7. e.g. Deut. 15:12-15
8. Jenkins, 2011 p.21-22
9. Prov.13:34

6. Can the Violence be Justified?

There are various arguments put forward to justify, excuse or simply ignore the violence attributed to God in the bible. None of them satisfactorily address the problem.

Don't rock the boat

Why does much of "popular theology" seem to ignore the glaring discrepancy between the violent warrior God depicted in much of the Old Testament and the loving compassionate, self-sacrificing God we see in Jesus?" Throughout Christian history, there *have* been people who questioned the literal truth of God's supposed acts of violence but their views were not widespread. "Don't make an issue of it; just accept it as it is. Don't ask awkward questions, don't upset people's faith, don't make it complicated." This used to be a common approach (and still is).

To a large extent, we don't read the worst verses; we sanitise the stories for popular consumption. This is misleading and dishonest. We know the damning events are there but we choose to ignore the problem. However, ignoring problems does not make them go away. Things brushed under the carpet make cleaning up harder in the long run; skeletons in cupboards tend to rattle. However, there is hope. A growing number of people are rightly not satisfied with this approach and want to ask the "awkward questions."

At the same time, many attempts have been made to excuse or justify God's violent actions.

Genuine explanations

For some of the actions described that are contrary to God's nature, there *are* fairly straightforward explanations.

For example, think about the numerous accounts of plagues and illnesses described as punishments from God inflicted on individuals, groups and nations in bible stories.

Eruptions of infectious diseases have always occurred. There would, no doubt, have been many devastating epidemics in biblical times over the centuries, Some particularly memorable ones would have been talked about and remembered. Thousands of people did die in this way but that does not mean that God sent the plagues, any more than he sent the coronavirus in 2020 – (though, no doubt, there will be some people who think that). The ancient people interpreted it in that way because that is how they reasoned at that time. They knew nothing about germs and viruses. They believed that God was directly responsible for everything that happened and so came to the conclusion that an epidemic must be a punishment for something that displeased him.

These events only remain a problem if you want to believe that all the accounts are literally true and God did deliberately send hideous plagues to kill thousands of people. Plagues happened. People attributed them to God. That is how people thought. That is what they wrote. We now know they were wrong; God would never have deliberately sent illness or natural disasters to punish people.

Other natural explanations

It has been common to try to give other "natural" explanations for many of the offending events. Most of the Egyptian plagues could have been based on naturally occurring events in that time and place, though much exaggerated and hardly likely to follow so soon after one another. We could even imagine that the difference in something such as diet could account for the Israelite slaves not getting a disease which affected many Egyptian households. In the story of the crossing of the Red Sea, it might be suggested that although people could walk across the sea bed, the heavy Egyptian chariots got bogged down in the mud. There are different suggestions for the site of this crossing, some making it more plausible as a seasonal tide.

However, the whole point from the writer's point of view is to say that this is God's story. It is great storytelling. It is God's triumph over the great and powerful Egyptian empire. It is God's action to rescue his chosen people.

Finding loopholes to take God out of the equation does not change this. This is the way that the writers and compilers believed God would behave but that does not mean they were right. This is what has to be challenged. The God we see in Jesus would not so manipulate natural forces to drown an army. That is not the way God works.

A warrior God

It is a sad fact that human beings have a propensity to violence and fighting over land. Territorial disputes are common from neighbours to nations, needlessly destroying the lives of individuals and whole communities. Life in the ancient Near East was no exception. The lands of the bible were in a strategic position constantly fought over and conquered by one imperial power after another. War was brutal and life was precarious and fragile. Ethnic groups and smaller nations fought for their continued existence and they still do. It is not surprising therefore that there is a lot of fighting in the biblical accounts. It would be unrealistic if it were not so.

The problem comes when God is portrayed as an enthusiastic protagonist in all this death, destruction and land grabbing. We should find this shocking. We should want to shout, "No, that can't be true!" We have already described how many nations at that time believed their gods would fight for them in battles and that victory gave glory to the god.

Jesus completely rejected the idea of the warrior messiah that people hoped for. He prevented his followers from violently resisting his arrest.[1] In the sermon on the mount it is the peacemakers who will be called children of God.[2] Jesus taught, "Love your enemies and pray for those who persecute you."[3] So these aggressive, destructive acts would always have been wrong, and I believe we dishonour God if we suggest otherwise. God does not compromise his integrity. He would never have been "a warrior God."

The end justifies the means

What about the conquest of Canaan and God's intention that the Israelites should possess the "Promised Land?" There have been plenty of commentators who say that it was appropriate for God to act in that way at that time. It was necessary to achieve the objective. It was for the greater good. (Pity about the collateral damage.) They say that God meeting people where they are means that he accommodates his behaviour to fit in with the beliefs of the time, so it could then be true that he did lead them as the warrior God they expected.

However, the supporters of this theory are usually eager

to say that God does not act in that way today. This argument assumes that God's behaviour has changed. God does not accommodate humans by behaving like them. He does not do so now and never did. His moral values do not change from one age to another; he is the same, yesterday, today and forever. Christian teaching is that God acts in love and is changeless and totally dependable.

Jesus never compromised his position. He constantly gave radical teaching and acted in ways that challenged the customs and beliefs of his time. This got him into trouble with the authorities and ultimately led to his death. God would never have lowered his standard of behaviour to suit the human expectation or culture of the time.

The Canaanites were evil

The argument is often put forward that the Canaanites were really evil. They practised child sacrifice and other "abominations" or deserved destruction just because they fought against the Israelites instead of relinquishing their land. They deserved to die. God was right to punish them.

However, there is no real reason to believe that the Canaanites were particularly worse than any other nation and it was the Israelites who were the invaders! In reality, the Canaanites just happened to be the ones who were in the way. Again, to accept this argument that the Canaanites were justifiably punished for their supposed evil requires that God's essential nature has changed. It is still common practice today to promote fake news about those who stand in your way, in order to discredit them and justify your own actions.

Even if the Canaanites had been evil, would the God we see in Jesus have chosen to annihilate them as described?

We are told that God continually forgave the Israelites for their failures. Jonah believed that God wanted to forgive the people of Nineveh.[4] According to the prophet Ezekiel, God says, "Have I any pleasure in the death of a sinner, and would I not rather that he should turn from his wickedness and live?"[5]

Jesus preached repentance and forgiveness. It was a major feature of his ministry and message. The disciples were to forgive, "seventy times seven times."[6] It is also found in the Lord's Prayer, "Forgive us our sins as we forgive those who sin against us." [7]

Killing those who displeased him has never been God's way of tackling evil.

Those big numbers

Numbers in general in the bible are not too reliable in terms of factual accuracy. This was never the writer's main concern. Some characters are said to have lived to fantastic ages. It is often a sign that they were considered important. The bible gives particular significance to certain numbers. How often do we come across seven, twelve, or forty? So when describing battles, some commentators, wanting to play down the damage to God's reputation, suggest that the numbers are greatly exaggerated. This may be true. It was the custom for military leaders to magnify their achievements. Inscriptions from other nations have been discovered which illustrate this. The Moabite Stone (also called the Mesha Stele), dated around 840 BC, was discovered in Jordan in 1868. The inscription describes King Mesha's victory over Israel in greatly exaggerated terms, claiming that "Israel has perished forever." It clearly had not. Also, the size of the armies or the number of people killed in battles seems out of all proportion to the populations likely to have been involved. Furthermore, letters of the Hebrew alphabet were also used as numbers, so it would have been easy to make mistakes. Discrepancies can easily occur when manuscripts are hand copied.

This is an example of how many errors can occur in the texts. The book of Samuel says that on one occasion King David defeated 700 chariot teams.[8] In the same event in Chronicles the figure is 7,000.[9] Another example is the age at which Jehoiachin became king. According to Kings, he was eight years old but in Chronicles, he was eighteen. So for various reasons, numbers are not very accurate. Casualties may well have been fewer and civilians may have had time to run away.

Nevertheless, true as all this may be, it does not alter the basic principle. It will not do as a means to exonerate God's supposed actions. It does not alter what the authors chose to write. If God deliberately killed or ordered the death of even one person, he is acting contrary to his divine nature as seen in Jesus. Either God ordered mass murder or he did not. A few hundred more or less does not change the principle. Mitigating circumstances are irrelevant.

Kill the women and children

What attitude should we take to the specific orders to kill women and children? Are we supposed to believe that God really ordered that? Some argue that it was necessary to kill the women, as the text claims because they would corrupt the Israelite men and lead them into worship of foreign gods. The children of evil people would grow up to be evil people themselves. At all costs, the Chosen people must be kept pure. That does not say much for the faith of the Israelites. Could they only be kept faithful by removing the temptation? In any case, it did not work because the Israelites continued to worship other gods.

As noted before, worship of other Canaanite gods such as the Baals and Asherah, the Canaanite gods thought to control the weather and fertility, constantly got the Israelites into trouble. Most nations believed that there were many gods who had their areas of influence. They were capricious, uncaring, quarrelled with each other and had to be placated and persuaded to help human beings. The Israelites believed their god was different. He cared for them and would protect them as long as they were faithful. They came to believe that he was, in fact, the only god but there is evidence that for much of the time they wavered between seeing him as the greatest of the gods rather than the only one. Their food production was very weather dependent, so it was tempting for some to hedge their bets. Being tempted away to worship other gods is a recurrent theme throughout the Old Testament and is constantly given as the reason for Israel's downfall.

All the slaughter, including that of the women and children, failed to prevent this, so the reason given for killing them is not a valid one. Nor does it fit with the nature of a just and peaceful God.

God can do as he likes

Some people say that if God is God he can do as he likes but this would make him no better than the "other gods." It would make him no better than a selfish human being. What God likes is to love. He can not act against his nature. Some people say that if the bible says God did something then he did, and if God did it, it must be OK. So since when was mass murder ever OK? What kind of moral value are we working on? What kind of God does this envisage? Again, this is making human beings more moral than God. If we keep our eyes on Jesus such thinking is impossible. Jesus willingly endured the cross. God must remain faithful to his nature.

Gracious as well

Another argument is that we should balance the "good God with the bad God" and allow that both exist in God's nature. We will look at many of the good laws in a future chapter and, of course, God is also shown as forgiving, loving, patient, generous, compassionate, merciful and wanting his people to show the same attitudes towards one another. However, if God can also be mean, jealous, destructive and vengeful, he is no better than human beings and not someone we would want to worship.

At the risk of being repetitive, that is not what we see in Jesus. God does not have a Jekyll and Hyde personality. We cannot use the bible as a whole as a clear moral guide. It does not present a consistent picture and we should continually be aware that not everything the bible says about the character of God is true. We must read all of the bible through the lens of Jesus to determine which actions are likely to be true and which are not. If they are not a true representation of God's character, we should be prepared to discount them.

God's justice?

The next argument put forward is that God had to act with justice; disobedience must be punished and the punishments were deserved. The argument about how God acts in the world, such as, "Do the good prosper and evil suffer?" will be discussed below when we consider the story of Job. God demands justice, as in fair treatment, for all who are poor and oppressed. The violent actions we are talking about in this issue are not just. Think back to the stories of God's punishments. They are harsh, cruel, oppressive and arbitrary.

A hymn from the nineteenth century by Frederick William Faber expresses the idea that the judgement of men is harsher than that of God:

> "There's a wideness in God's mercy, Like the wideness of the sea:
> there's a kindness in his justice which is more than liberty.
> There is no place where earth's sorrows are more felt than up in heaven:
> there is no place where earth's failings have such kindly judgement given.
> But we make his love too narrow by false limits of our own:
> and we magnify his strictness with a zeal he will not own.
> For the love of God is broader than the scope of the human mind,
> and the heart of the eternal is most wonderfully kind.
> If our love were but more simple, we should take him at his word;
> and our hearts would find assurance in the promise of our Lord."

Authors who are reluctant to discount God's involvement in the violent actions are often keen to insist that we should not follow that example today. The trouble is that we do. It is wrong now and was wrong then and we need to say that it was. Throughout history, horrendous things have been done in the name of God. The influence has not gone away. Some people seem quite keen on the idea that God will punish wrongdoers so long as they are sure that it will not include them.

The prophet Nathan tells King David a story about a rich man who steals his poor neighbour's only lamb to feed his guest.[10] David is enraged until he realises that it is really a picture of his own behaviour. He had put Uriah in a situation where he would be killed in order to cover up his adultery with Uriah's wife, Bathsheba. The Israelites were happy for the prophets to pronounce God's judgement on the other nations until the tables were turned on themselves (as in Amos 3:1). Jesus warned people not to judge others while ignoring their own faults. "Why do you see the speck in your neighbour's eye, but do not notice the log in your own?"[11] Jesus' focus on repentance and forgiveness has already been discussed.

For all the above reasons, I find the traditional arguments for accepting and justifying the violent acts of God to be unconvincing and incompatible with the nature of God as seen in Jesus.

Notes

1. Jn.18:10-11
2. Mt. 5:9
3. Mt. 5:44
4. Jonah 4:2
5. Ezek. 18:23
6. Mt. 18:22
7. Mt. 6:12
8. 2 Sam. 10:18
9. 1 Chr. 19:18
10. 2 Sam. 12
11. Mt. 7:3

7. Eroding Authority?

Here we come to what seems to be the main concern that many people have with simply saying that God did not do all the things the bible says he did. It is a common belief that God decided and approved all the content of the bible even if he did not actually write or dictate it and so people feel reticent about questioning or criticising the morality of what happens. They feel like they are criticising God.

There is also a belief held by many people that to challenge the literal truth of some biblical events is to deny the authenticity of the bible and gradually erode it away, destroying people's faith with it. A dramatic preacher started to tear out lumps of the bible which it had been suggested were not literally true. "What have we got left?" he demanded triumphantly. I do not wish to tear anything out. I am not suggesting that we should remove anything from the bible. I *do*, however, want to interpret differently some of what is there. Properly understood, the bible is not eroded by a less literal approach. Quite the opposite. An interpretation which takes account of scholarly study and research into the composition of biblical texts, ancient historical records, new developments in translation, archaeology, etc., actually sheds light on many problems. It enables some difficult issues to be resolved. It can remove misconceptions that for many people are *obstacles* to faith. It is enriched in meaning, and is better able to speak to people in the twenty-first century who have not grown up with a biblical tradition. The bible gains a much wider meaning and impact when it is better understood. It is not diminished by realism. God can speak to us through its words just the same. Everything happens in a context and events and interpretations can be much better understood if we know what that is. We recognise that knowledge in all areas of life changes our perspective. This should also be true for the bible. We do not see God as people saw him two to three thousand years ago. *If we challenge statements in the bible, we are not challenging God, we are challenging what the ancient Israelites thought about God.* And we should do that. The bible gives us permission to do that. (This will be explored in Part Two.)

If we insist on taking everything literally, we get into ridiculous problems about trying to explain the sun standing still[1] or donkeys[2] and snakes[3] talking or the logistics of Noah's ark.[4] As part of a story with a meaning and things to teach us, these events do not present a problem. The things on which some people base their faith, like the inerrancy or infallibility of the bible, are obstacles to others. Some cling to the idea that everything basically happened as the bible says. To others, this seems impossible and out of touch with reality and modern knowledge. They might feel that the only thing eroded is common sense.

The danger is that we can make the bible itself into an idol. The bible points us to God. We worship God, not the bible. Some people are horrified if you make notes in a bible or put a battered falling apart one into recycling. They revere the book itself, the object because it contains the message of God. Some thought processes go like this: "The bible must be right, even when our logic and moral compass says that the action it describes is not. If only we could understand, it would all make sense because God's thoughts are not our thoughts. There must be some theory of everything where every story and statement has its place, even genocide, if only we could see it."

People who think like this want a neat, tidy and non-controvertial way of interpreting the bible but that's not realistic; we need to apply the logic we would use in other areas of our lives. We need to open our eyes and our minds and use our God-given powers of reasoning. We must not try to force the bible to be something it is not. It is no good trying to shut the difficulties in a box, close the lid and insist that no such difficulties exist.

The bible won't disintegrate into dust if we ask realistic questions and apply the moral instincts that God has given us. God will still be there and he will be free of the damaging images we have given him. The inspiring purple passages of the bible will still be there. Above all, the message of Jesus and the Kingdom of God will still be there and it will be stronger. If we scrape the barnacles off the hull of the ship it will sail better. "The bible is not in itself so much a compass or a chart, as directions for finding the pilot, and he it is who will be to us both compass and chart and steer us through," quotes Briggs.[5] Don't let us make the bible into an idol that we can't question. Don't let us be afraid to denounce those parts that don't fit with the message of Jesus.

Decisions, decisions, decisions ...

Many questions in life, both large and small, in private and in public concerns, do not have a perfect solution. We often have to choose between what we might call the lesser of two evils or try to decide which decision will cause the least harm. I am writing this during the coronavirus pandemic as we begin to come out of lockdown. The big issue is, do we risk more lives by coming out too early, or damage more people's mental health and risk job loss and financial breakdown by continuing? No solution will be best for everyone.

Similarly, we have difficult decisions to make about the bible. Ever since research into background information on the bible began, Christians have been divided on how this should influence the way we read and interpret the bible and how it might affect our faith. Does it change the authority we give to the bible? Does it affect the truth of its message?

Many people feel that questioning the authority of the bible, as traditionally interpreted, undermines people's faith. However, many other people are *deterred* from faith by the violent image of God (and other issues) that a traditional view presents.

If we take the position that the bible cannot be wrong, we are saying that God *did* order genocide and *did* wipe out thousands through plagues in anger and vengeance. Alternatively, if we believe that God *did not do these things*, we have to compromise or abandon the notion of the bible's infallibility.

Many authors sit precariously on the fence on this issue. They do not like either alternative. I jumped down from the fence many years ago and nothing that I have read since has tempted me to climb back. It is the nature of God that is of supreme importance and has to be defended. God *is* Love and cannot act contrary to his nature.

Important long-term issues are at stake here.

1. Having a correct image of the character of God.

2. Preventing God's so-called actions being used as an excuse for violence in our own time or condoning such use in the past.

3. That we present a true image of God, the bible, and Christianity to the world and the next generation.

I believe it is time for Christians to state categorically that God did not send a flood to destroy the world, or kill

Egyptian babies, or zap Israel's enemies, or slaughter thousands for disobedience, or condone rape or all the other horrific acts for which the writers of the Old Testament tell us God was responsible.

I have been told we cannot "just say this" but I believe that the bible itself gives us permission and even demands that we do. The message of Jesus demands that we do.

If we know someone well, we do not readily accept stories about them which seem out of character. We say, "He wouldn't do that. It's not in his nature." If we can say that about a human person, surely we can say it of God, whom we believe to be the essence of love, unchanging, forgiving, trustworthy and completely dependable. If we accept the nature of God as shown in the teaching and actions of Jesus, how is it possible to believe that a few centuries earlier his policy had been to wipe everyone out in a very cruel way and start again – or to order wholesale genocide – or to kill children for the crimes of their parents? Such behaviour would be totally inconsistent and incomprehensible by human standards, let alone God's. The God we meet in Jesus would not have sent death and destruction to demonstrate his power.

So we have a complex problem to solve: If God did not do these things, why does the bible say that he did? This is a very logical and commonly asked question which requires a complex answer.

There are huge misconceptions in much common understanding of what the bible is and what it teaches. These often lead to rejection and disbelief. The answers to some basic questions can radically alter the impression we have of the bible. Who wrote it and when? How was it put together? What was the intention of the authors? How did the culture of the times influence their beliefs? What was their physical understanding of the earth? Was the world made in six days? Did God order genocide? Does God support war or slavery or the subordination of women? Is everything literally true? Does God agree with everything the bible says? Traditionally we have often not been encouraged to ask these questions but they are of vital importance to understanding the real messages of the bible.

We now need to explore these questions to give us a basic understanding of the underlying issues involved. The image of the bible we need involves many interlocking factors which it is difficult to separate. In a detective story, several investigated strands, at first seemingly unconnected, come together to build the final solution. Hopefully, our exploration of different aspects of the bible may work in a similar way. We explore these strands in part two.

Notes

1. Josh. 10:12-13
2. Num. 22:28-30
3. Gen. 3:1-5
4. Gen. 6 & 7
5. Briggs, 2003, p.113

Part Two
Building the Picture

1. Where Did the Bible Come From?

What we know and believe about the authorship and construction of the bible is one of the very significant factors influencing how we see and understand the bible as a whole, including how we view the violent aspects of God described in the Old Testament. What are our expectations as we read?

God did not write the bible. It did not materialise from heaven gift wrapped in non-disputable facts, tied with angelic certainty ribbon and stamped with God's seal of approval! The bible gradually evolved over centuries of storytelling, remembering, imagining, exaggerating, believing, doubting, debating, hoping, revising, arguing, recording and eventually compiling, although that in itself took several hundred years. Much was originally passed on from generation to generation through oral tradition.

Think of visiting a library and walking around the different subject sections. Now select a few books from each section: ancient mythology, history, philosophy, poetry, prayer, family saga, ancestry, historical novels, letters, laws, drama, church doctrine and ritual, and religious beliefs. Choose sixty-six of the best of these and arrange them in a row on a bookshelf. This gives us some idea of what the bible consisted of before it all got bound into one volume. Except that they did not actually exist as books as we know them because the printing press and bookbinding had not been invented. Old Testament texts were written on scrolls made of different materials and copied laboriously by hand. There were therefore not many copies, they were very expensive and most people could not read. The scrolls would be read aloud in the Temple and synagogues for people to hear. There was probably a wider selection than we have in our bibles. A choice was gradually made by considering which were thought to be the most valuable and useful. Over time, the texts were revised, re-revised, and different versions of the same or similar events amalgamated, changed and edited. Older material, like ancient poems, were inserted into newer accounts.

Mistakes in copying inevitably occurred. For example, when books had begun to be typeset and printed, there is an English bible printed in 1631 in which the seventh of the Ten Commandments reads, "Thou *shall* commit adultery." When the mistake was discovered, most were collected and burned but a few survived.

Compiling the Old Testament

The final version of the Hebrew bible was agreed on and compiled in three sections, at different times.

The Pentateuch, or Torah, the first five books of the Hebrew bible, consisting of Genesis, Exodus, Leviticus, Numbers and Deuteronomy was probably put together in its final form around the fifth century BC. This was considered the most important part of the sacred Scriptures for the Jewish faith and practice.

The second section is the collection of the books of prophets. These were Joshua, Judges, Samuel, Kings, Isaiah, Jeremiah, Ezekiel and what we still refer to as, "The Twelve Minor prophets" which are found at the end of our Old Testament. These are thought to have become an established part of the Hebrew Scriptures around the second century BC. However, they existed in the form of separate scrolls, not as one book.

These two collections are what is referred to in the New Testament as, "The Law and the Prophets".

The remaining books to become accepted were agreed

on much later and collectively called, "The Writings."

The "Christian" Old Testament has mainly kept the same books as the Hebrew bible but re-arranged the order in which the books are placed in the bible.

Compiling the New Testament.

The message of Jesus was passed on by word of mouth. Lists of stories and sayings were probably written down. Leaders like Paul wrote letters to groups of converts that had been built up in different areas. These would have been passed around and some became particularly valued. When the first disciples began to die it was necessary to record their knowledge and the Gospels began to be written. There were more than the four we have in the bible and some of these still exist but they were not chosen by the early church to become part of the scriptures.

Selecting the twenty-seven books that now make up the New Testament took some time and discussion with cases being made for the inclusion or exclusion of certain books. The final selection was not formally agreed on until 393 AD at the Synod of Hippo and confirmed in 397 AD at the third Synod of Carthage. The New Testament as we know it today then came into being.

Language and translation

Needless to say, the bible was not originally written in English! The Old Testament was written in Hebrew and the New Testament in Greek. Jesus spoke Aramaic.

We know from reading Shakespeare or Chaucer how much language changes over time. Words change in meaning. An obvious example is the word "gay". It used to mean bright and happy. "The child who is born on the Sabbath day is bonny and blithe and good and gay," says the poem. Several other words in that sentence have also mainly gone out of use.

There are always problems in translating from one language to another because there is often no one word that exactly conveys the same meaning. It is not always possible to work out the exact meaning of a word in an ancient language which is no longer spoken. The same word can have different associations in a different culture. There are words commonly used in Yorkshire which are not understood in Bristol. How many differences in terminology can you think of between Britain and America? If you learned French you were probably caught out by words that appear the same but have different meanings. All this is relevant to the issues involved in translating the bible. It is not immune from problems and mistakes because it is the bible.

The gospels were written in Greek because Greek had become the common language of that part of the world and dispersed Jews spoke Greek. The Greek translation of the Old Testament was the one most frequently used. The originals had no punctuation or chapters and verses. These were added later and some interpretive choices had to be made. To make things a bit more complicated, Hebrew was written without the vowels, so could only be understood and translated as part of its context. Some bibles have notes offering different translations of certain words as found in different manuscripts.

The bible was later translated from the Greek into Latin, the official language of the Roman Empire, and the first bibles in England were in Latin. There were some early translations of certain books into English but most ordinary people never had any opportunity to read the bible for themselves. John Wycliffe translated the bible from Latin into English in the 14th century but the church declared it illegal and people were executed for possessing a copy. Until then, all copies were handwritten, and therefore rare and expensive anyway. It was not until 1456 that the first printing press was invented.

In 1526, William Tyndale made a new translation of the New Testament into English from the original Greek. This was printed in Germany and smuggled into England. Tragically, Tyndale was arrested and executed.

Amazingly, only a few years later, the Coverdale bible, the first full bible printed in English, was allowed and could be used publicly in churches. "The Authorised Version" / King James bible followed in 1611. A large proportion is the work of William Tyndale.

This was "The bible" until the late 19th century.

There are now over a hundred different translations of the bible in modern English.

They take advantage of further developments in interpreting and translating from ancient texts. While some keep to a direct translation, others paraphrase into more contemporary language. There is even a version of the gospels in the Yorkshire dialect!

So the whole process by which our bible came to us was a very human one. Yes, no doubt God inspired countless people along that journey but nevertheless a very involved and gradual human process. It also required expertise and painstaking research in studying and translating ancient languages. The motivation was not just religious. It involved intrigue, power politics and persecution alongside faith, patient determination and courage.

2. Contradictions

A further significant aspect of the composition of the bible is that it is full of contradictions, inconsistencies, repetitions and differences of opinion. This too affects how we should see the bible as a whole. The bible is quite happy with these differences. The compilers of the bible seem to have been quite happy with these. They did not edit them out or try to smooth them over. This says a great deal about what the bible actually is and what it is not.

We might like to have a neat package of reliable consistent teaching and rules direct from God which we could follow without question or controversy. Some people do try to regard it like that but they must be reading a different bible from the one that I have.

What we do have is a record of many people's experiences and a growing understanding of God over many centuries. They represent many changing, developing and often conflicting ideas and beliefs. We can believe that they were to varying degrees inspired by God but through their human experience and within their cultural contexts. We can see very different concepts of the nature of God and what he wants and values. The differences are an integral part of the exploration into God that the bible records. Consequently, there is not just one consistent image of God in the bible. It spans about one thousand five hundred years of beliefs in changing circumstances so why would we expect them to be the same? Ideas have changed and evolved over the centuries.

So there are many views expressed in the bible that are not necessarily those of God. There are many actions and emotions attributed to God which are incompatible with the nature of God that we see in Jesus.

Some people want to believe that everything in the bible

is literally true but at a very basic level, this is not possible. There are many conflicting accounts of events which cannot be harmonised. We should not tie ourselves in knots trying to harmonise them but accept what is there as different people's contributions.

For example, right at the beginning of the bible, there are two separate creation stories. They have considerable differences, therefore cannot both be literally true.[1] If we look carefully at the flood story, we can see that two versions have been woven together. How many animals went into the ark? Was it one pair of each or seven pairs of each?[2] We often do not notice these discrepancies and from a faith point of view they need not matter but it is important to acknowledge that they are there and not try "to iron them out." That is how the bible is. It is a human book. The compilers, editors and revisers thought it right to include the differences and the varying points of view and even the arguments. They make the bible realistic in a way that a rigid and censored version would not. God can and does work with it as it is.

Adapting history

The books of Samuel and Kings tell the "history" of the Israelites from the end of the time of the Judges until the time of exile in Babylon. They include the prophets Samuel, Elijah and Elisha, the decision to have a king, the reigns of the famous kings, Saul, David and Solomon, building the Jerusalem Temple and the division of the kingdom into Israel in the north and Judah in the south. Then follows accounts of all the kings of both countries until the fall of the northern kingdom to the Assyrians and the fall of Judah to the Babylonians.

The books of Chronicles are an alternative version of

this history. Much of the story is the same but the writer wants to give a positive message to people returned from exile who may be of another generation who have never seen their own land. Most ancient people lost their identity when they were defeated and taken over by a greater power. They became assimilated into the new nation and culture. This happened to the northern tribes. The Jews in Babylon, however, managed to retain their identity as a people because of their faith in God and adherence to their unique features of circumcision, Sabbath observance and food laws. They needed to believe that God had not forgotten them. They were still his people despite all that had happened and God would eventually restore their fortunes. Chronicles portrays a picture of the past that the Israelites should aspire to and describes the great kings David and Solomon as much more idealised characters. It leaves out the more disreputable episodes in their lives. For example, David's adultery with Bathsheba and the arranged death of her husband. Also, much of the problematic relationship between Saul and David and the difficulties David has with his sons are left out, as are Solomon's many foreign wives and his worship of other gods in later years. It omits much of the history of the northern kingdom which no longer existed. Great importance is placed on building the Temple for the glory of God. Chronicles gives a different slant on events to suit the time of writing.

Another obvious discrepancy is the taking of the Promised Land. Did Joshua conquer the whole land as stated in the book of Joshua or was it a much more gradual process as stated in Judges? (cf. Chapter 3 above.)

Does God change his mind?

"Is God a mortal that he should change his mind?" the prophet asks.[3] After the people made and worshipped the golden calf, God was angry and declared that he would destroy the Israelites and begin again with Moses (as with Noah). Moses pleaded for the people and "The Lord changed his mind about the disaster he had planned to bring on his people."[4]

It is interesting that Moses, in this case, is portrayed as more compassionate than God, as is Abraham when he pleads for the people of Sodom and Gomorrah.[5]

There are many other examples in which God appears to change his mind in the course of the Old Testament. Starting from a belief that God controls everything, it is logical to suppose that God has changed his mind when conditions change. However, the Christian belief is that God does not change his mind. Ideas and beliefs about God change but God remains the same. His values and intentions do not change.

The bible updates itself

Rules change to meet the changing needs of society in different times, as do ours.

For example, Deuteronomy updates the laws in Exodus and Leviticus on a number of issues such as slavery and marriage.

Were you allowed to be married to two sisters at the same time? Jacob had married both Leah and Rachel.[6] However, the rules in Leviticus later say not.[7]

Sacrifice was an important part of worship but where could it happen? On many small, local altars,[8] or only in the one designated central place?[9] Again, the beliefs and rules changed over time and situation.

Should Israel have a king? We first meet the possibility of a king in Deuteronomy.[10] It looks forward to a time when the Israelites will be settled in the new land and says that they may have a king of God's choosing, if they want one. Clearly written with hindsight, it warns a future king not to be self-seeking and make himself rich at the expense of his subjects. He must be diligent in observing the law of God. At the end of the time of Judges, the people do ask Samuel for a king. They want to be "like other nations."[11] Samuel warns them of the danger that a king will oppress them with taxes, military service, slave labour and favouritism for his family and friends. God warns that they are rejecting *him* as king in this request.[12] The people still ask for a king. In what seems to be a separate story, Saul is chosen and anointed by Samuel.[13] This probably reflects a long, very human, debate over the issue. In later years, Samuel's predictions all came true. Issues of succession caused much division. Solomon amassed great wealth and worshipped other Gods. The nation was becoming divided, the rich dominating the poor in a way that had never been intended.

Discrepancies in the New Testament

If we move to the New Testament, we can also find plenty of discrepancies and differences of opinion. It is not possible to harmonise all the events recorded in the four gospels, including accounts of Jesus' birth and resurrection. This does not matter. It is not an obstacle to faith. The four accounts agree on the essential Christian beliefs. Do you ever disagree in your family about exactly when a particular thing happened? My husband and I have different memories about exactly where we were when we got engaged. As we have been happily married for 46 years it hardly matters! Memories of similar and regular events blend together in our memories over the years. I doubt that the disciples kept a diary. In any case, the gospels are literary compositions. The writers each selected their material, probably from a variety of verbal and written sources. Events are grouped together or placed in a particular order to make a point. The significance was more important than factual detail or geographical accuracy. St John writes, "… these are written so that you may come to believe that Jesus is the Messiah, the Son of God, and that through believing you might have life in his name."[14] This is surely the aim of all four gospels. The opening of Luke's gospel says that he selected his material from various sources that were available in order to, "write an orderly account."

What Paul says in his letters does not always tie up with the sequence and details of events told in the Acts of the Apostles. There are two completely different accounts of how Judas Iscariot died.[15] There was obviously huge disagreement about how Gentile believers were to be incorporated into the faith.[16] The disciples had the advantage of actually being with and learning from Jesus and receiving the Holy Spirit. But they still misunderstood and disagreed among themselves on some important issues. The disciples at first believed that the world as it was would end in their lifetime. Jesus challenged and updated many Old Testament laws and customs as in the sermon on the mount.[17]

So it is impossible to read the bible at length without encountering these disagreements, discrepancies, contradictions and updates. They cannot all be literally true and they cannot all express God's opinions. We shall now move on to thinking more about what we mean by Truth, another very significant issue in how we interpret our bible.

Notes

1. Gen 1:1-2:3 and Gen 2:4-25
2. Gen 6:19 and 7:2
3. 1 Sam 15:29
4. Ex 32:14
5. Gen 18
6. Gen 29
7. Lev 18:18
8. Ex 20:24
9. Deut 12:13-14
10. Deut 17:14-19
11. 1 Sam 8:5
12. 1 Sam 10:19
13. 1 Sam 9
14. Jn 20:31
15. Mt 27:3-5 and Acts 1:18
16. e.g. Acts 15
17. Mt 5

3. Is it True?

What is truth?

Pilate asked Jesus, "What is truth?"[1] and libraries of books have been written to debate this question. There are clearly different kinds of truth. Queen Elisabeth was crowned in Westminster Abbey on 2nd June 1953. This is literally true. A verifiable event happened to a certain person, on a certain date, in a certain place. This tends to be what people have in mind when they ask, "Is it true?" about some incident in the bible. However, even a literally truthful account would differ, depending on the experience of the witness. If everyone at the coronation wrote an account of their memories of the day, they would all differ in some way. There would be different experiences, different opinions, different feelings, and different details remembered. A member of the royal family would have very different memories from a young rather bored child, squashed into a neighbour's sitting room watching a twelve-inch black and white TV. The bible compilers were willing to include multiple versions of the same events.

Great truth can also be told in fiction. For example, there was never a boy called Oliver who asked for more. He is a fictional character in a story. But Charles Dickens' book told the awful truth about the ill-treatment of children that was common in institutions at the time. More recently, in his novel, *A Thousand Splendid Suns,* Khaled Hosseini uses fictional characters to tell the truth about the treatment of women under the Taliban in Afghanistan. *Watership Down* uses the adventures of a bunch of rabbits to illustrate different types of regimes and forms of government. Our literature is full and overflowing with such examples. All worthwhile fiction embodies something that is true about real life. Human beings have always made up stories to talk

Is it True?

about important aspects of life. Long before writing was invented, people of all places and cultures told stories and passed them down the generations. Where did we come from? Why are we here? Why is there so much evil in the world? Where did it come from? Why do we speak different languages? All ancient cultures have their own myths and legends which try to address these timeless and universal questions. Some of these are found in Genesis. The creation, the Garden of Eden, Adam and Eve,[2] the tower of Babel,[3] and the Flood, are all examples. They contain huge amounts of truth about God, human nature and our human condition but they are not, and were never meant to be, *literally* true. For some reason, our bible reading and religious teaching have tended to treat these stories as if they were literally true events in history. By insisting on this, we often get a wrong impression of the bible and the character of God. We also greatly reduce their value by restricting their meaning and encourage the image of Christians as people who "believe six impossible things before breakfast"[4] and are out of touch with modern thought.

Fiction can tell the truth in a powerful and dynamic way. Many would read or listen to a story who would not read a theological study or a political theory.

Docudramas are popular. They bring the news to life by adding details and conversations that put flesh on the event and engage in a way that a brief headline may not. Interviews with people actually involved help us identify and sympathise with an issue much more than a generalised, impersonal statement.

Jesus understood the power of stories; a lot of his teaching was in the form of parables. The Good Samaritan[5] and The Prodigal Son[6] have become common phrases in our vocabulary. Most people do not worry that these are not literally true. We automatically think about what they are meant to teach us. Jesus did not usually explain the meaning of his stories. He left people to think and work it out for themselves. He often did not give "straight" answers to questions or replied with another question. He constantly used figures of speech to illustrate and give emphasis to his teaching. "If your foot causes you to stumble, cut it off."[7] Old testament writers also told stories with a message, notably Job and Jonah. Many "historical" episodes can also take on a more general meaning and significance. Some convey religious doctrine or political propaganda.

"It's in the bible, so it must be true" needs to change to, "It's in the bible because it has truths to tell us." This kind of truth can be translated into truth for all times and places and be relevant to different cultures. The readers of bible times knew this. They did not ask, "Is this true?" so much as "What are we meant to learn from this?" The idea that truth must be literal and factual is limiting and misleading.

Finding truth in myth
Begin reading carefully at the beginning of Genesis and it is immediately apparent that there are two different stories of creation following one behind the other. They were written at different times; perhaps 400 years apart. The historical situations were different and the authors had different reasons for writing, with different messages to convey. The first was probably written when the Israelites were a conquered people, living in exile in Babylon. It was a general cultural belief at the time that if you were defeated, it was your god who had been defeated by the god of the victor. The Genesis story affirms the Israelite's

Is it True?

god as the supreme creator. He will not be defeated by anyone.

These writers had no idea how the earth actually came into being. They were not there. God did not give them 21st-century knowledge of science and cosmology. They were not writing Science. The structure of earth and sky envisaged is how it seemed to them. After all, that is what it looks like. The sky does look like a dome with rotating sun, moon and stars. They were using poetry and story to express important truths which are timeless. Here are some of the ideas we can see in the first creation story.[8]

1. "In the beginning, God." God was there before the Big Bang, before the planets were formed, before organisms began to form in the oceans; the original scientist, artist, inventor, craftsman, a bringer of life. Whatever his part in creation and whether it took six days or six thousand million years, the story affirms, "In the beginning, God."

St John echoes Genesis when he begins his gospel, "In the Beginning" affirming his belief that Jesus has always existed, all one with God.

2. Creation is good. Despite the mess humans have made in so many ways and the damage we have done to our planet, creation, as God intended it, was always meant to be good. It can be mended. This is the chorus of the poem, "God saw that it was good." We have an amazing, often beautiful, wonderful world.

3. Human beings are made, "In the image of God." We cannot be sure exactly what that meant. It does not mean we look like him (God does not have a visual appearance), or that we have all his attributes or exist in the same way. I believe it means primarily that we have a capacity to love; a spark easily diluted or smothered but also inspiring great

selfless acts and lives, a spark in every human being, a touch from God, who is the essence of pure love.

4. As the most intelligent form of creation, at least in this corner of the universe, we are responsible for caring for each other and the world, as responsible stewards. Its future is in our hands. We have been forced to realise this most forcefully in recent years.

5. In this story, men and women were created equal.

This creation myth is not *literally* true, but it expresses timeless truths.

The second creation story, beginning in Gen. 2:4 goes on to tell the story of Adam and Eve. These are not individual people. Adam was not a man's name. It is derived from a Hebrew word meaning humankind. Eve was not a woman's name. They represent everyone. They are the story of humanity and what happens when God is disobeyed. They suggest how evil and suffering came into the world. Possibly the original "passing the buck" story. Humans have always been good at this; it's always someone else's fault. "The man blamed the woman, the woman blamed the snake and the snake didn't have a leg to stand on!"(Seen on a poster outside a church) But seriously, women have been suffering from the effects of that story ever since. The author of 1 Timothy uses it to legitimise the subordination of women.[9] "… For Adam was formed first, then Eve, and Adam was not deceived but the woman was deceived and became a transgressor." We need to think about why stories were chosen and told as they are.

People have always asked ultimate questions about life and its origins and all ancient communities made up their stories to "explain" where they came from. As long ago as the 3rd century AD, Origen, a Christian scholar, said that the Old Testament creation story was not to be taken literally. "Scripture is not speaking here of any temporal beginning, but it says that the heavens and the earth and all things that were made were made 'in the beginning,' that is, in the Saviour." *Homilies on Genesis 1.1*

Some things are outside the capacity of human beings to grasp. Sometimes we are favoured with glimpses of insight which seem to be there for a second and then melt away; an intangible something. Our fingertips touch but we can't grasp the concept. There are ideas beyond human logic or experience. Bible authors acknowledged this. Isaiah tells us God says, "For my thoughts are not your thoughts."[10] St Paul asks, "For who has known the mind of the Lord?"[11] and wrote to the believers in Corinth, "Now we see in a mirror darkly..."[12] That does not mean that we should not keep looking and reaching out. This is what biblical authors did. It is what can be expressed in story and myth and poetry: A burning bush that is not consumed. A valley of dry bones come to life. A still small voice. A vision of angels. They try to define God, sometimes genuinely seeking the truth, sometimes to suit their own ends and find it is not possible. But collected clues and insights come together to make a patchwork of beliefs, ideas and experiences, remembered, treasured and recorded.

What about Christianity and science?
There should be no conflict between Christianity and science. They represent two aspects of our world which are both correct and complement one another. If I take a picture of the front of my house and then another of the back, I have two different views. This does not mean that one is wrong. They are both pictures of my house but seen from a different perspective. If I want to give someone an accurate idea of what my house is like, I need to show them

both pictures and prove that they meet in the middle! Some atheist scientists tell us that the photo of the front of the house is the only true photo. The back does not really exist; religious belief is just a figment of our imagination or wishful thinking.

Sadly, some Christians insist on telling us that the back of the house is the only real picture. Young Earth creationists insist that the world was literally made in six days, evolution is a delusion, the world is no more than 6000 years old and that the dinosaurs, if they really existed, lived alongside human beings.

Both these atheists and these Christians are wrong and present a distorted picture of the truth.

It is unfortunate that from the beginning of the period of the Enlightenment, religious officialdom rejected much scientific discovery. This has had a tragic and long-lasting effect on the relationship between Christianity and science. In 1632, Galileo Galilei was convicted of heresy for saying that the earth revolved around the sun. He had asserted in 1609 that his observations of the planets through his newly developed telescope confirmed the theory put forward by Nicolaus Copernicus' in his publication, *On the Revolutions of the Celestial Spheres,* in 1543. In 1613, Galileo wrote that the bible was an authority on faith and morals, not science. It was not until 1992, that the then Pope, John-Paul II, formally acknowledged that those who had condemned Galileo were wrong.

Following the publication of Charles Darwin's *Origin of the Species* in 1859, theories of evolution were immediately rejected by some church authorities because they were thought to threaten the authority of the bible by questioning the literal truth of Genesis. Sadly, this view still quite widely persists.

The fact that some Christian groups want to continue this division between religion and science is damaging the image of Christianity in the eyes of non-believers, many of whom tend to think this view represents the belief of Christianity as a whole.

So truth in the bible, as elsewhere in literature, is much broader than literal fact and we damage the reputation of the bible and distort the image of God if we do not acknowledge this. From the myths of Genesis to the parables of Jesus, the bible is packed with truth expressed in story and poetry. To view the bible in this way is another of our key factors in interpretation.

Notes
1. Jn 18:38
2. Gen 1-3
3. Gen 11:1-9
4. From *Through the Looking Glass* by Lewis Carol
5. Lk 10:29-37
6. Lk 15:11-32
7. Mk 9:45
8. Gen 1:1-2:3
9. 1 Tim 2:9-15
10. Isa 55:8
11. Rom 11:34
12. 1 Cor 13:12

4. A Definition of History

Another challenging topic and a further strand in our detective story is how we should understand history in the Old Testament. This is particularly significant for how we see the destructive acts of God. The books of our Old Testament from Joshua to Chronicles are generally referred to as history but we need to consider what is meant by this. It is worth remembering that in the Hebrew bible, most of the books we call history are actually classed as prophets.

There is no such thing as completely objective, totally accurate history. All history is, to some extent, coloured by the person who writes it, even when their intention is to be honest. Everything is written or told from someone's point of view. Many régimes have rewritten their official history to suit their ideology or protect their reputation. Undesirable episodes are left out or given a fresh slant. This happened in the bible too. We have already seen an example of this in the books of Samuel and Chronicles. We are learning to look at our British colonial past with new eyes and recognise how much exploitation and ill-treatment of indigenous populations were involved. Everything connected to the slave trade has been re-evaluated. Some once honoured characters are now seen in a different light.

Twenty-first century history teaching in British schools focuses on examining and comparing different sources and looks at events from varying perspectives. It is understood that there is not just one unchallenged record of events.

History has been interwoven with legend and folk law. For instance, Charles Stuart (Bonnie Prince Charlie) who made a bid for the English throne in 1745, was a real figure in documented history but the many romantic stories, poems and songs his memory inspired have moved into legend. Accounts with origins in real events have been embellished. Legends have always grown up around the memory of famous people. These are rooted somewhere in actual events but the stories which come first to mind in popular culture are often those embellished by imagination. Ask people what they know about King Alfred and the chances are that the first thing that comes to mind is the story of burning the cakes. Figures such as King Arthur and Robin Hood probably never existed but the ideology attached to them is a part of British heritage and identity. It is very likely that similar things would have happened in recounting the lives and exploits of some bible heroes as their stories were passed down the centuries.

Some people see the whole bible as an accurate record of historical events but the authors of the bible books, traditionally classed as history, were not setting out to write objective, unbiased history. They had a very positive agenda. They were writing a religious document with an important message: the Israelites are God's chosen people.

5. The Chosen People

"You are a holy people to the Lord your God: it is you the Lord has chosen out of all the peoples on earth to be his people, his treasured possession."[1]

The Israelites are God's chosen people and the Old Testament is their story. The story of how this came to be and what it means for their history as a nation. It is a saga spanning centuries, through the victories and defeats, triumphs and disasters, the good times and the bad. The thing that was constant: Yahweh was their God and he cared for them to the exclusion of everyone else. He would defend them against their enemies. He would guide them in his ways of righteousness and holiness. This is the core of Old Testament faith and the focus of their recorded history.

The story begins in Gen 12 with the call of Abraham. He is to leave his present home and journey to Canaan. God promises, "I will make of you a great nation" and that his descendants would be as numerous as the stars in the sky.[2] Through a complicated ritual, God makes a covenant (agreement) with Abraham[3] that his descendants will be given all the land of Canaan.

Problems of childlessness, displacement through famine and years of slavery in Egypt seem to threaten this prediction but at last, we arrive at the story of Exodus where God overcomes the power of Pharaoh and the might of Egypt and empowers Moses to lead the Israelites out into freedom in the wilderness of Sinai. Moses goes up the mountain and God tells him to instruct the people

"If you obey my voice and keep my covenant you shall be my treasured possession out of all the peoples. Indeed the whole earth is mine but you shall be for me a priestly kingdom and a holy nation."[4]

The Chosen People

Then follows the Ten Commandments and several chapters of laws which are to govern all areas of Israelite life. There is no division between religious and secular laws; they are all seen as coming from God. God will bless the nation with good health, abundant crops, wealth and prosperity and victory over their enemies.

But there is a catch! Too good to be true? Blessings are balanced by curses of horrendous proportions heaped up one upon another, (actually over 50 verses of them!)[5] if Israel does not keep her side of the bargain. They must obey God's commandments, particularly: THEY MUST NOT WORSHIP OTHER GODS.

Curses are not the total end of the story. There will be the possibility of restoration after repentance.

This belief in their position as God's chosen people is reflected in the way the remainder of Israel's history is interpreted and written. Everything is said to be controlled by God for a reason, nothing is random. Joseph forgives his brothers for selling him into slavery, telling them that it was all part of God's plan. "It was not you who sent me here but God."[6] Throughout the conquest of Canaan and afterwards, success or failure is believed to be determined not by the size or skill or strategy of the armies but by whether or not the Israelites were obedient to God. God gave them victory if they were faithful. He allowed them to be defeated if they were not.

Centuries later, the Israelites' warrior God must still be acknowledged as the real hero in all the battles. In a time after Joshua when the Israelites are settled in Canaan, they are led by a series of "Judges". These are supposedly wise people chosen by God. One of these is Gideon. When Gideon is preparing to fight the Midianites, he is told to drastically reduce the number of troops to 300 men. The people must not think that they have won the battle through their own efforts. It is God who gives them the victory.⁷

A regular pattern follows through this series of leaders. The Lord appointed a judge and all was well for a time. When the judge died the people "did what was evil in the sight of the Lord," mainly worshipping other gods. God was angry and allowed other nations to conquer them. The Israelites "cried out to the Lord" and he appointed another leader to rescue them. When he died, the cycle started all over again. It follows the pattern suggested by the covenant between God and the Israelites described above. Disobedience, disaster, repentance, restoration. This can describe the whole of Old Testament "history."

Moving on into the much later period, when Israel has become a kingdom, the same theory prevails. After King Solomon there follows a succession of kings who are all judged to have been good or bad kings depending on whether they allowed Israel to fall into the worship of other gods.

As an example, King Ahaz "did not do what was right in the sight of the Lord." He sinned by making images of the baals and so the Lord "gave him into the hand of the king of Aram." They were defeated and many people were killed or taken captive. It was all seen as God's punishment for disobedience.⁸

When eventually the Northern kingdom falls to the Assyrians and later still the southern kingdom is conquered by the Babylonians and the people taken into exile, it is all God's doing. He has allowed Israel to be defeated because of her unfaithfulness to him. They have repeatedly broken the covenant. The theory never wavers. In the Old Testament, history is understood through the lens of this core belief and written accordingly. This is how the Israelite authors explain how the promise to be the chosen people has seemingly gone so wrong. Obey God and the nation will prosper, disobey and disasters will follow.

Deuteronomy even goes to the length of saying they should kill members of their tribe who try to tempt them to follow other gods.[9] (Duet. 13:6-9,17:2-5)

So a chosen people, but chosen for what?

Was it just to remain as they were: an exclusive group with special privileges, keeping what they had for themselves? Maybe expanding their territories? Perhaps most people were satisfied with that or just took it for granted, but there will always be visionaries who ask questions and see beyond the immediate to the wider implications of a belief system, in this case, that of being a favoured people.

One such visionary was the author of the Book of Jonah.

Did this supreme and powerful God who had made the whole world really only care about one small nation or were the Israelites special because they were to have an important task? Were they to share the knowledge of this God they had come to know and trust, with other nations? Perhaps God actually cared about them too.

Jonah: reluctant missionary

The story is well known. God tells the prophet Jonah to go and pronounce judgement on the people of Nineveh, the capital of Assyria, for all their evil ways. After a failed attempt at running away, via a ship going in the opposite direction and a big fish (the bible never calls it a whale), Jonah arrives in Nineveh. Contrary to Jonah's expectations, the king and the people listen to his message, take it seriously and repent. They put on sackcloth and ashes, which is what people did in those days to show that they were really, really sorry about something. God is pleased and merciful and decides not to destroy the city after all. Good result. But not as far as Jonah is concerned. Jonah is very unhappy and disgruntled. He complains that he always knew God would go and be merciful in the end and those terrible Ninevites would not get what should be coming to them! As far as Jonah is concerned, they are still the long-standing hated enemy. God asks,

> "Should I not be concerned about that great city in which there are more than a hundred and twenty thousand people who do not know their right hand from their left, and also many animals?"[10]

Rather nice that the animals get a mention. This is in sharp contrast with the divine order to slaughter them all back in Jericho and not forgetting all those who drowned in the flood!

Jonah is a brilliantly told story with the message that God cares for everyone, including Israel's enemies. It contrasts with the traditional view expressed by the prophet Nahum who had predicted that God would destroy the city.[11] Perhaps also with the popular opinion but certainly with the policies of Ezra and Nehemiah which we will come to later in this chapter.

Ruth

The book of Ruth is a beautiful story about caring and faithful relationships. Its message is in line with that of Jonah.

When the Israelites were travelling through the wilderness before reaching Canaan, an incident is described in Numbers 25 in which Moabite women led Israelite men to worship other gods thus provoking God's anger. It's a gruesome story.

Ruth by contrast is described as a good, kind and faithful person despite being a Moabite. She is a young widow who leaves her own country and clan and follows her mother-in-law to Bethlehem, accepting Yahweh as her God. Her loyalty is rewarded. She is treated kindly and marries a leading Israelite who is her late husband's relative. It is probably the most peaceful book in the Old Testament and comes nearest to seeing events from a woman's point of view, though still in a system governed by the laws of men. The story ends with a genealogy where we discover that Ruth (a foreign woman from a despised tribe) is the great-grandmother of the great King David.

Those foreign wives
The story of Ruth and its message is in sharp contrast to the views expressed in the books of Ezra and Nehemiah regarding foreign wives. Perhaps Ruth was written partly in protest against this. The people who returned from exile in Babylon and are starting to rebuild Jerusalem, have brought with them many foreign wives. Ezra sees this as a terrible disgrace. He collects all the people together and, after lists are made of everyone involved, most agree to send away their foreign wives along with their children. We are not told where they are supposed to go or how they are to be supported. The chosen people must be kept pure.[12]

Nehemiah also rails against those who have taken foreign wives, reminding the people of God's original laws.[13] This is part of a larger campaign to return to a stricter observance of the rules and customs that set Israel apart from the rest of the nations.

The Chosen People and the New Testament
The early church believed and taught that Jesus was the long-awaited Messiah and that the Old Testament prophecies were fulfilled in him. He was the continuation and fulfilment of Israel's story and mission. This was not a

Disowning the Violence

new faith which contradicted the Jewish concept of the chosen people but was the next part of the story which completed God's promises to Israel. In Jesus' life, death and resurrection there is a new covenant which makes some of the original laws and rituals unnecessary. The disciples did not stop being Jews, rather they saw that it was the task of the Jews, having been prepared through the centuries, to now take their God out into the wider world.

In his last words to the disciples according to Matthew, Jesus said, "Go therefore and make disciples of all nations."[14] Matthew includes many Old Testament quotations which he claims are fulfilled in Jesus. He wants to prove to the Jews that Jesus is indeed the Messiah. The problem was that to most people the expectation of the Messiah was that he would be a military leader who would drive out the Romans and restore Israel to independence. They still wanted their warrior god. Jesus did nothing in words or actions to suggest this idea and told Pilate, "My kingdom is not of this world."[15]

At Pentecost, the disciples were given the ability to preach in many languages to all the people who were gathered in Jerusalem.[16]

However, Problems arose over receiving Gentiles into the Christian faith. Foreigners who wished to embrace the Jewish faith had always been welcome but they had been expected to be circumcised and obey the Jewish law. Now it was suggested that Gentiles becoming disciples of Christ should not have to do this. It is evident from Acts[17] and some of Paul's letters, particularly Galatians, where he uses some very strong language, that this was a highly controversial issue which caused a lot of trouble and dissension. Some leaders such as James felt strongly that converts should, in essence, become Jews first. Paul argued vehemently against this policy.

Peter had a vision in which God told him to eat creatures that according to the law were "unclean" and not to be eaten. When he protested, God said, "What I have made clean you must not call profane." Peter was puzzling about this when three Gentile men arrived, asking for him. Then Peter realised the meaning of the vision and agreed to go with the men. On arriving at the home of Cornelius, a centurion, Peter said, "You know that it is unlawful for a Jew to associate with, or visit a Gentile, but God has shown me that I should not call anyone unclean. I truly understand that God shows no partiality, but in every nation, anyone who fears him and does what is right is acceptable to him."[18]

A light to the Gentiles
Back in the Old Testament, Isaiah had described Israel (the people as a whole) as a servant of God, saying, "I will give you as a light to the nations, that my salvation may reach to the ends of the earth."[19]

When the prophet Simeon holds the one-week-old baby Jesus in the Temple, he predicts that Jesus will be, "A light for revelation to the Gentiles and for glory to your people Israel."[20] St Paul later quotes this on more than one occasion in his preaching. Paul wrote to the Gentiles in Ephesus assuring them that they were completely accepted by God, as all, both Jew and Gentile are united as one body in Jesus and the promise of the Gospel is for everyone.

Many Jews chose to believe and follow Jesus but most of those in authority in the synagogues did not, so the "followers of The Way" became separated and were persecuted by the leading Jewish authorities. It appears that Paul always went to the synagogue first when he went to a new place but regularly the traditionalists in authority opposed his teaching and stirred up hostility. (For example, in Acts 14 at Iconium.) Many Gentiles readily accepted the message of the Good News of Jesus and Christianity as it came to be called spread around the Mediterranean.[21]

This "chosenness" of the Israelites and the debate about its meaning and where it was leading, is a constantly important theme throughout the bible. Prophets had warned that Israel's place would be given to others if she was unfaithful.

Jesus told the parable of the vineyard.[22] Isaiah had already told a similar story.[23] The original tenants, (the Jews), reject the owner (God) and kill his son (Jesus) so the vineyard is given to others. The chosen people have not recognised Jesus and failed to fulfil their mission to be a light to the world. Matthew tells us that the chief priests and scribes understand what Jesus is saying but it makes them even more opposed to him.

Jesus says he has sheep who are not of this fold, thereby including people from outside the Jewish race. "I must bring them also and they will listen to my voice. So there will be one flock and one shepherd."[24]

This is an ongoing debate
Some Christians today think that people who are not Christians are excluded from inclusion in God's all-embracing love. Some even want to say that certain kinds of Christians who do not share exactly the same beliefs as they do are excluded. They see themselves as "the chosen people" whom everyone else must join, or else suffer rejection. Some early Christians argued, "Unless you are circumcised according to the custom of Moses, you cannot be saved."[25]

Certain accepted formulae of belief today have become

the new "circumcision" in the eyes of those who hold them. They believe that you can only be "saved" by being a Christian who accepts a very specific set of beliefs. This would exclude the majority of the world's population.

Jesus does not recognise any man-made boundaries and distinctions. He asked people to look for the Kingdom of God, which includes anyone who values, or could learn to value, the things valued by God. Jesus taught his disciples to pray, "Your Kingdom come, your will be done, on earth as in heaven."[26] This is what the message of the whole story of the bible is heading towards. It continues into the lives of Christians today and into the future times to come. According to Matthew, in his last words to his disciples just before his ascension, Jesus said, "Go therefore and make disciples of all nations." [27] There is no room for racism, favouritism or any form of exclusion in the message of Jesus. The Israelites were given knowledge of God as a gift to share with the world.

Chosenness for any selfish and exclusive reason has been firmly updated. The authors of Jonah and Ruth had understood this in a way that many other Old Testament writers did not.

So throughout the Old Testament, what may be referred to as "history" is not a straightforward, factual, unbiased record of events. It is a record of a people's struggle to exist and a search for God and their attempts to work out how these two things fit together. Their story is written from that point of view. It incorporates evolving ideas, and constant debate, with contrasting beliefs on religious practices, politics, ethics, justice, suffering and the nature of God and what he desires. It reflects the changing cultural life of the ancient Middle East through more than a thousand years. We are given the developing images of God as these people imagined him, rather than a reliable picture of the true nature of God. For this, we have to wait for Jesus.

Notes
1. Deut. 14:2
2. Gen. 15:5-6
3. Gen. 15:7-21
4. Ex. 19:6-7
5. Deut. 28
6. Gen. 45:4-8
7. Jud. 7
8. 2 Kings 16
9. Deut. 13:6-9,17:2-5
10. Jonah 4:11
11. Nah. 1:1, 3:7
12. Ezra 10:10-44
13. Neh. 13:23-27
14. Mt. 28:19
15. Jn 18:36
16. Acts 2:5-12
17. e.g. Acts 15:1
18. Acts 10
19. Isa 49:6
20. Lk 2:22-24
21. e.g. Acts 13:48-49
22. Mt 21:33-41
23. Isa 5:1-7
24. Jn 10:16
25. Acts 15:1
26. Mt 6:10
27. Mt 28:19

6. Is Suffering a Punishment for Sin?

The story of Job

The belief system of the Israelites was that good people would be rewarded in this life and that bad people would suffer. We have seen how this was thought to apply to the fate of the nation.

The story of Job challenges this theory. Job is a wealthy farmer who has all the good things in life: happy family, land, animals, good income. Satan says that Job only worships God because he is so well off. He would lose his faith if his fortunes changed. God disagrees but allows it to be put to the test. Disaster after disaster robs Job of his family and possessions and he becomes very ill. However, he remains faithful to God. Three friends visit and through very long conversations, try to convince Job that all his suffering must be the result of sin. He needs to confess and ask forgiveness. They stick to the simple conventional wisdom of the time. Job keeps insisting that he has not committed any great sin, he is innocent and demands to know why he is being punished unjustly. Eventually, God shows up in chapter 38. His answer is a majestic and powerful literary acclaim of the splendour of His creation. It's impressive poetry, but it does not at all answer Job's question. It is more like an old-fashioned school teacher saying, "How dare you ask that question?" God does agree that Job is innocent and the friends are wrong and restores his fortunes with new family and possessions. (Hard on the original family and animals!) The question is out there: What about the good people who suffer and the bad people who prosper? The traditional theory does not match the facts.

Job is every person who has ever asked, "Why do bad

things happen to good people?" – a universal and timeless question that in this life can never have a completely satisfactory answer. (Which is probably why the author of Job does not attempt to give one.) God's nearest answer to the question is found in Jesus' life, death and resurrection, but that was still to come. In Job, the supposed pact between God and Satan, the Accuser, is a literary device for creating the scenario of the story. It's great fiction. If it were literally true, it would not say much for the morality of a God who would play with someone's life in that way.

The New Testament agrees with Job

St. Paul certainly did not follow the view that those who do God's will have physical good fortune. He gives a long list of his sufferings in 2 Corinthians 11.22, but insists (Romans 8) that, "Nothing in all creation can separate us from the love of God in Christ Jesus."

Jesus is of course the supreme example that this theory is not true. He was the best person who ever lived but he died a terrible death. He warned his followers that discipleship would involve suffering.

Sins of the fathers.

Another significant belief about the character of God and his dealings with people threads its way through the Old Testament. It is a further aspect of the reward and punishment theme that was questioned in the book of Job.

It must have been evident that some people behaved badly but seemed to get away with it. So a theory evolved as a way of explaining why this could happen. Instead of deducing that their theory must be wrong, they found a way to get around it: Judgement must be deferred to future generations.

The concepts of God's judgement and anger on the one hand and God's mercy and forgiveness on the other, are in constant balance and contrast.

In Exodus we read how God supposedly describes himself as:

"A God merciful and gracious, slow to anger and abounding in steadfast love and faithfulness for the thousandth generation, forgiving iniquity and transgression and sin, yet by no means clearing the guilty, but visiting the iniquity of the parents upon the children and the children's children, to the third and fourth generation." (Exodus 34:6-7)

This belief is echoed in many Old Testament texts. For example, while still a child, the prophet Samuel receives a message from God that he is to pass on to Eli, his teacher. Eli's sons had behaved badly and Eli had not prevented them. Punishment will be postponed into the future. "On that day I will fulfil against Eli all that I have spoken concerning his house. For I have told him I am about to punish his house forever."[1]

Again, in the time of the Kings of Israel, King Ahab and his wife Jezebel worshipped other Gods and ordered the murder of the prophet Naboth because he would not give them his vineyard. Because Ahab repents (more fasting and sackcloth and ashes) God says, "I will not bring the disaster in his days but in his son's days, I will bring disaster on his house."[2]

In another story, King David and Bathsheba's baby son dies because they had committed adultery in conceiving him.[3]

Of course, we know today that actions and lifestyles and the way children are brought up and any number of situations have future consequences. The histories of families and nations are affected by what happened in the past but we would not now think that it was God's judgement that caused this. However, in the faith system of the Israelites, God controlled everything, so if a bad person did not seem to suffer it was reasoned that this could be the explanation.

Whole families were often punished for the action of one person as in the story of Achan, for example. (cf. Part 1, Chapter 2.)

It was not always the view in the Old Testament that people would be punished for the sins of their ancestors. We can also find proclamations that say the opposite.

Deuteronomy updates Exodus (as quoted above) in this respect. "The fathers shall not be put to death for the children, nor shall the children be put to death for the fathers; every man shall be put to death for his own sin." [4]

Some prophets also endorse this latter view. Ezekiel explains at great length a message he has received from God. He gives lots of specific examples which boil down to, "It is only the person who sins that shall die." [5] "For I have no pleasure in the death of anyone, says the Lord God. Turn then, and live." [6]

Jeremiah has the same message as he looks forward to a future time when people will have a closer relationship with God.[7]

So, as in other areas, opinions within the bible differ and develop. The idea that suffering could be a punishment for sin was still around when we get to the New Testament. When Jesus brings sight to a man born blind, his disciples ask: "Teacher, whose sin caused him to be born blind? Was it his own or his parents' sin?" Jesus replies that it was nothing to do with either.[8]

Jesus undoes the link between sin and suffering entirely

in some of his teaching. Matthew records Jesus saying, "Love your enemies and pray for those who persecute you so that you may be children of your father in heaven; for he makes his sun rise on the evil and on the good and sends rain on the righteous and the unrighteous." [9]

On this question of the link between punishment and sin, therefore, there is no single consistent theory in the bible. As in many theories concerning God's nature and way of working, it changes over time.

We can all be very good at selecting the evidence that suits our theories and rejecting or ignoring the ones that don't! It can be misleading and dangerous to quote some individual bible verses without reference to their context or the overall message of the bible. The bible includes all voices. It does not select one view and remove the opposition. It preserves the differing stages of the debate. Again, to decide what is more likely to be God's opinion, we must look to Jesus.

Notes
1. 1 Sam. 3:12-14
2. 1 Kings 21:29
3. 2 Sam. 12:14-15
4. Deut. 24:16
5. Ezek. 18:4
6. Ezek. 18:32
7. Jer. 31:29-30
8. Jn. 9:2-3
9. Mt. 5:44-45

7. Great Storytellers
Talking with God

There are many passages in the Old Testament which profess to record the direct speech of God and many of these demand violent actions which are destructive, harsh and harmful. Because they have been taken literally, as the "voice" of God, or "The Word of the Lord," they have been used to support and justify the use of violence around the world, throughout recorded history. Examples were given in chapter 2. I suggest that much of this reported speech is actually a clever literary device.

The bible tells of its heroes having long conversations with God in which they were given complex, specific instructions and messages. Did this really happen? Did they actually hear God's voice with their ears in a literal sense, or is this just the storyteller's way of describing the experience? I do believe that there are times when God actually speaks to people but probably not often using long two-way conversations. When someone says: "God told me...", what they more often mean is that a thought came into their mind, and they believe it came from God. It might have, but then again it might not. There are many other influences that affect us: the age in which we live, our whole culture and upbringing, our own personalities, our desires, ambitions, experiences and concerns, and the kind of religious teaching we have had. These all play a part in what we believe about God, and what he might be saying to us. *There is no automatic and foolproof system for filtering out God's influence among all the others.*

If it were possible to look into the minds of a million people to discover their concept of God, the result would be one million different pictures. There is no single image of God accepted in all detail by all Christians, let alone those of other faiths. In many cases, the description would reveal more about the person than it would reveal about God. Mistakes must be constantly being made about what we believe God wants, otherwise there would not be so much disagreement within the churches, nor would so many different Christian denominations have evolved.

All this was most likely just as true for the Israelites as it is for us, but the style of relating the stories tends to camouflage this fact. We tend to think and talk about and retell these Old Testament stories as if there were no doubts involved, and as if these conversations with God were as obvious and concrete as between two human beings. Some of these writers were excellent storytellers. Conversation makes for a good, dynamic story. What better than a conversation with God? The thoughts, doubts, worries, questions, convictions, hopes and fears which go through the persons' minds are all put into the form of a dialogue with God, making great tellable, and later, readable drama. If every time the Old Testament says: "God said..." we were to substitute, "Moses (or whoever it was) believed that God was telling him to..." it would be less dramatic but we might have a much more realistic impression of what really happened.

Many bible writers use dialogue as part of their art of storytelling. In the New Testament for instance we have Jesus having a conversation with the devil.[1] Was the devil really present with Jesus in the wilderness or do the temptations represent some of the ideas that Jesus considered as he prayed and worked out how he was meant to fulfil his future ministry? Jesus was a brilliant storyteller. Throughout his ministry, he taught in striking parables and constantly used dramatic and exaggerated figures of speech to make his points such as, "If your hand or foot causes you to stumble, cut it off and throw it away."²

It is hard to visualise anything that is completely outside our own experience. So we are bound to make many mistakes about what we believe to be the will of God and what he is saying to us and what he is telling us to do. It is impossible for us to have a complete overview. It's as if we exist in one piece of a jigsaw without having the picture on the box. It can be hard to work out where our piece fits into the whole. The bible tells us we are made in the image of God, but too often we make God, or our idea of God, in the image of human beings. We imagine that God would react in the same way that we would react in a given situation. We need to look carefully at Jesus. The Old Testament composers lived before Jesus and could not have the insights which Christians can gain from seeing God revealed in him. The biblical writers were aware of our human limitations. On the whole, they did not try to hide the mistakes of their heroes. The Old Testament family sagas rival the TV soaps for melodrama: murder, adultery, jealousy, rivalry, revenge, hatred, trickery, betrayal... it's all there! But God, too, is often seen in human terms. He is frequently depicted as having the same reactions and emotions as the human beings who populate the stories.

For example, in a story told in 1 Kings:22, God plots murder by inviting someone to feed false information to the prophets who will advise the king so that he will make a wrong decision and die in battle! This all comes to pass in a convoluted tale with another gruesome ending. "And the Lord said, "Who will entice Ahab, so that he may go up and fall at Ramoth-Gilead?"³

You might remember that in contrast, King David was *condemned* for a similar action when he sent Uriah into battle, hoping that he would be killed.[4]

Another example where God is said to deliberately lead people astray is when he is often said to, "harden people's hearts". A well-known example is when the Egyptian Pharaoh refuses to let the Israelite slaves leave the country. God is said to have "hardened his heart" on several occasions.[5]

Another example is Joshua's attacks on Canaanite towns, when we are told: "For it was the Lord's doing to harden their hearts so that they would come against Israel in battle, in order that they might be utterly destroyed, and receive no mercy, but be exterminated."[6]

If we accept these varied quotations as the actual words of God, we are asked to believe that God enticed people to make wrong decisions which were immoral, unwise and dangerous.

Creating an image of God

The bible constantly uses metaphors, signs and symbols. These are literary devices which are not meant to be understood literally.

Bible stories, hymns, meditations and sermons in use today, constantly talk about God as though he has the same sort of body as a human being. It is of course reassuring and true to sing, "He's got the whole world in his hands," although we know that God does not actually have hands. He can "see" without having eyes and "hear" without having ears. When it comes to God's actions, it is important to remember that these are metaphors and not assume that God reacts and behaves in the same negative human ways that he is frequently portrayed as doing in the Old Testament stories.

Disowning the Violence

It is difficult to think purely in the abstract. The Israelites had this problem. The second of the Ten Commandments says they are not to make images of God. It was natural for people to feel the need for something visual and worshippers of other gods in the surrounding countries had images representing their gods. We hear constant stories of the Israelites as a whole, or individuals, being enticed into the worship of these. The histories and the prophets regularly record this as the main reason for Israel's failures and defeats. We often feel the need for something concrete to hang on to as a focus of our belief and a visual sign for others and so signs and symbols are adopted. For instance, the symbols of the cross and the fish have become important to Christians. In Old Testament times, the Israelites thought that God needed a home. It was really that they needed a focus for their worship, so they built physical symbols in the form of the tabernacle and the ark of the covenant, containing the Ten Commandments, which travelled with them through the wilderness and years afterwards as an assurance of God's presence with them. It became a revered and holy object.

According to the account in Exodus 25-27, God himself gave detailed instructions for the ark's construction (as in the case of Noah's ark). God said, "And have them make me a sanctuary, so that I may dwell among them." Great care was needed in approaching God. The ark must not be touched. It was to be carried on long poles. On one occasion during the reign of King David, when the ark was being carried triumphantly to Jerusalem, the oxen pulling the cart stumbled. Uzzah put out his hand to steady it, a seemingly natural and instinctive act we might think, but he was struck dead. The bible says that God was angry that Uzzah had touched the ark and death was the immediate punishment. It is yet another of the many harsh punishments attributed to God. Even David, we are told, thought this unjust and was angry with God![7]

Much later, huge resources in expensive commodities and manpower went into building the elaborate Temple which they believed to be a fitting place to glorify their God and be the place where they would gather to worship and offer sacrifices. Over the years, some Israelites came to realise that God did not need these. Solomon recognises this.[8] God did not live in buildings or holy objects. Again we see that beliefs and ideas are constantly changed and challenged within the bible.

Jesus teaches us that God cannot be confined anywhere. He is not confined to the words of the bible and does not conform to all the images with human traits and values that its authors mistakenly choose to give him. This particularly applies to the multiple acts of violence and cruelty which are attributed to God in so many Old Testament stories.

Notes

1. Mt 4:1-11
2. Mt 18:8
3. 1 Kings 22:19
4. 2 Sam 12
5. Ex 10:1-2
6. Josh 11:20
7. 2 Sam 6:6-8
8. 1 Kings 8:27

8. The Law and the Prophets

Does the extensive system of detailed laws, sacrifices and festivals decreed in the Old Testament show us a true picture of the character of God? If we take the accounts as being literally true, most of them are his direct commands.

Moses was given the Ten Commandments on Mount Sinai after the Israelites were rescued from slavery in Egypt.[1] Some of them still form basic accepted rules for any civilised society. Over time, many more extremely detailed instructions were given to cover all aspects of daily life and worship. All rules were regarded as God's rules. There was no division between religious and secular. But they are not all constant. They are adapted and evolve down the generations to suit changing needs and opinions. The rules needed for wandering nomads were expanded and amended to suit a life settled in one place. It is another natural example of the human process of change and development. We have already seen examples of how Deuteronomy updates Exodus and how drastically Jesus updates much Old Testament law. Later in this chapter, we will see the radical understanding of some of the prophets. We have also seen how many laws demanded harsh punishments and discriminated against certain sections of society. It is hard to imagine these coming directly from God.

However, there were other laws that were good and enlightened for their time and situation and ethically and morally advanced in comparison with what is known in surrounding countries.

When Jesus taught: "Love your neighbour as yourself," he was quoting Leviticus 19:18. "You shall not hate in your heart anyone of your kin. You shall not take vengeance or bear a grudge against any of your people, but you shall love your neighbour as yourself."

Notice it says "*your* kin and *your* people" The interpretation of "neighbour" was quite narrow. Jesus famously extended the meaning of who should be regarded as a neighbour in the parable of the good Samaritan, where the hero is a despised foreigner, [2] and also in his teaching about having love for one's enemies. The Leviticus law just quoted did not include most foreigners and certainly not enemies but it was a good start.

There are many laws about helping some of those who are poor and disadvantaged:

"You shall not abuse any widow or orphan."[3]

"When you reap the harvest of your land, you shall not reap to the very edges of your field, or gather the gleanings of your harvest: you shall leave them for the poor and for the alien."[4] We can see this happening in the story of Ruth when she is encouraged to glean in Boaz's field, following the reapers.[5]

Similar passages refer to harvests of olives and grapes. "When you reap….it shall be for the alien, the orphan and the widow." [6]

"If you find a stray or injured animal you must help and return it to the owner."[7]

"When an alien resides with you in your land, you shall not oppress the alien. He shall be to you as a citizen among you: you shall love the alien as yourself, for you were aliens in the land of Egypt."[8] A resident alien was someone from another area who did not have his own land on which to grow food and widows and orphans were vulnerable if they did not have the protection of a male family member.

"When a man is newly married, he shall not go out with the army. He shall be free at home for one year to be happy with the wife he has married."[9] (It was important to have children to carry on the man's family line.) Members of our armed forces today might be pleased with that rule!

The biblical idea of "jubilee" was a radical innovation designed to prevent a widening gap between rich and poor and prevent families from sinking into debt. Every seventh year, debts were to be cancelled within the community and every fiftieth year, the Year of Jubilee, all ancestral land was to be returned to its original family. The clans were all allotted their areas of land after they settled in Canaan. The land belonged to God, the Israelites were the tenants.[10] A field was also to be left fallow every seven years.

The Christian Aid Jubilee 2,000 Drop the Debt Campaign to help the development of some of the poorest countries, was designed on this principle.

Israelites were not to charge interest on loans to fellow Israelites. Loans were a means of social support and not to be used as a money-making opportunity. "If you lend money to my people, to the poor among you, you shall not extract interest from them. If you take your neighbour's cloak in pawn, you shall restore it before the sun goes down; for it may be your neighbour's only clothing to use as a cover."[11]

The need for fair and unbiased judgements in disputes is also stressed. "Hear out the small and the great alike and don't be intimidated by anyone for judgement is God's. Do not be partial to the poor or defer to the rich."[12]

"You shall take no bribe, for a bribe blinds the officials and subverts the cause of those who are in the right."[13]

"You shall not pervert the justice due to your poor in their lawsuits. Keep far from a false charge and do not kill the innocent or those in the right, for I will not acquit the guilty."[14]

"You shall not be intimidated by anyone for the

judgement is God's."[15]

"Anyone who maims another shall suffer the same injury"[16] An eye for an eye or a tooth for a tooth [17] sounds barbaric to us but it was intended to restrict rather than encourage retaliation. You could not kill someone because they knocked your tooth out.

Honesty in trading was also important.

Slavery was very much an accepted fact of life in the bible but there were clear rules about the treatment of slaves which again were much better than those of other countries at the time. Slaves were not necessarily physically ill-treated. Someone could give his labour to repay a debt or loan or a thief could work as compensation.

"When you buy a male Hebrew slave, he shall serve you for six years but in the seventh, he shall go out a free person, without debt... If he comes in married then his wife shall go out with him." The downside was that if he married and had children while a slave, the wife and children would remain the property of the owner. He could choose to stay with them but he must then agree to be a slave for life. [18]

This is updated by Deuteronomy 15. The freed slave, "you shall not send out empty-handed, provide liberally out of your flock, your threshing floor and your wine press thus giving to him some of the bounty with which the Lord your God has blessed you... Do not consider it hardship because for six years they have given you services worth the wages of hired labourers."

If the owner knocks out a tooth or an eye of a male or female slave they shall go free to compensate for the loss.[19]

In Deut10:12-22 the attributes and moral values of God are summarised and to be mirrored in the fair dealings of his people. "So now, O Israel, what does the Lord your

God require of you? Only to fear the Lord your God, to walk in all his ways, to love him, to serve the Lord your God with all your heart and with all your soul, and to keep the commandments." (Deut 10:12)

We don't know to what extent these commandments were kept over the years but when we read the prophets there was clearly much corruption and lack of care for the poor and disadvantaged. These prophets question the importance of sacrificial rituals and religious festivals compared with the neglected need for social care and compassionate behaviour.

The practice of sacrifice
The practice of sacrifice formed a large and very significant part of Israelite religion but in time this too came to be questioned and criticised. Was this really the kind of worship that God wanted?

Sacrifice was important to many different cultures around the ancient world and it was the general practice of the ancient Near Eastern countries who were the Israelites' neighbours. The first seven chapters of Leviticus describe in detail all the different types of sacrifices that God is said to require. For the Israelites, the emphasis was on morality, holiness and purity. It was the way they maintained and renewed their relationship with God, a means of giving thanks and receiving forgiveness. Sacrifice was carried out with important rituals which seem barbaric and gruesome to us but were highly meaningful to those who performed them. They were an important and integral part of life, with prescribed sacrifices for all events and situations. In some types of sacrifices, the whole animal was burned as a gift to God. In fellowship offerings most would be eaten by the community as a symbol of renewed fellowship with God and each other. We still have fellowship meals and we still eat lots of animals. We just kill them out of sight and hopefully more humanely.

The need for social justice

In the later books of the Old Testament, we are introduced to the prophets. We tend to think of prophets as people who predict the future but the Old Testament prophets mainly spoke the truth about the present state of society as they saw it and as they fervently believed that God saw it. They were passionate about social injustice. They were not afraid to confront those in power. They looked back to the Ten Commandments and laws such as the ones quoted above, which they believed to be good. Israel had been designed to be a society with God as its leader, where laws were about being a caring society with provision for the poor and unfortunate. The prophets saw that in Israelite society there was little social justice. (Perhaps there never had been.) There was a growing divide between rich and poor and rulers had become corrupt and oppressive, growing rich at the expense of the general population through high taxes and tithes and an unjust legal system which favoured the powerful. Against this background, the elaborate rituals of worship and sacrifice had become hypocritical and empty gestures. They were not inspired by a love for God but had become an end in themselves, giving power and prestige to those in authority. The prophets taught that what God supremely cared about was how people responded to him and how they treated one another. "Love God and love your neighbour as yourself," had always summed up the law but how far had this been really applied?

Many of the prophets, in different time periods, all speak on behalf of God, saying:
"I hate, I despise your festivals, and I take no delight

in your solemn assemblies. Even though you offer me your burnt offerings and grain offerings, I will not accept them, and the offerings of well-being of your fatted animals I will not look upon. Take away from me the noise of your songs; I will not listen to the melody of your harps. But let justice roll down like waters, and righteousness like an ever-flowing stream."[20]

Hosea says: "I desire steadfast love not sacrifice, the knowledge of God rather than burnt offerings."[21] And the prophet Micah asks:

"Will the LORD be pleased with thousands of rams, with ten thousands of rivers of oil? Shall I give my firstborn for my transgression, the fruit of my body for the sin of my soul? He has told you, O mortal, what is good; and what does the LORD require of you but to do justice, and to love kindness, and to walk humbly with your God?"[22]

Isaiah complains:

"What to me is the multitude of your sacrifices? I have had enough of burnt offerings ...Who asked this from your hand?... I cannot endure solemn assemblies, your new moons and appointed festivals my soul hates... Everyone loves a bribe and runs after gifts. They do not defend the orphan, and the widow's cause does not come before them. They do not rescue the oppressed."[23]

And in the book of Proverbs, we read: "The Lord weighs the heart. To do righteousness and justice is more acceptable to the Lord than sacrifice."[24]

The prophets compared the ideal with reality and found it wanting.

These prophets would no doubt be criticising our

elaborate, materialistic Christmas celebrations beginning as early as October, and asking, "What does Jesus want for Christmas? Their answer would no doubt be, "Care for all the poor, homeless, abused and marginalised people in our world." Things have not, in essence, changed.

Jesus, of course, was highly critical of legalistic, uncaring attitudes. He clearly spent much of his time with all those rejected and neglected by society. He criticised the Pharisees for working out their tithes to the last pinch of herbs but failing to show love for God by acting justly.[25] One of the scribes who comes to question Jesus admits that to love God and one's neighbour is much more important than all burnt offerings and sacrifices.[26]

Jesus' inaugural sermon in Nazareth is about caring for those in need[27] and one of the last parables recorded by Matthew stresses that at the last judgement God will not ask how many ceremonies you have kept but whether you have cared for those in need.[28]

So we can see that the Israelites had a detailed set of laws and customs with elaborate festivals and rituals which governed their whole way of life which are presented as being ordained by God. Their relative importance changes with circumstances. Some were harsh and discriminatory and, over time, have been mostly rejected. Some were based on enlightened ideas which we still struggle to put into practice today. The prophets moved the emphasis away from ritual towards social justice, kindness and love and are surely more in tune with God's wishes. This is confirmed by the attitude of Jesus which we meet in the Gospels. (Comparisons between the Old Testament law and Jesus' attitude to people have been made in previous chapters.)

So among the detailed laws, customs and festivals of the

Old Testament, most supposedly given by God, there is a human mixture of good and bad, enlightened and savage. As in all societies, we see ideals that were not realised, as well as change and controversy. It is not possible that they were all given by the same God. By looking to Jesus, we can make our own judgements about which of these might most likely be endorsed by God and which would not. The whole picture presents a very human process through which people continued to worship God and seek his will and guidance. If the crucially important themes such as sacrifice can be challenged, so can the belief in a warrior God.

Notes
1. Ex 20
2. Lk 10:25-37
3. Ex 22:22
4. Lev 23:22
5. Ruth 2
6. Deut 24:19-20
7. Deut 22:1
8. Lev 19:33
9. Deut 24:5
10. Lev 25
11. Ex 22:25-27
12. Lev 9:15
13. Ex 23:8
14. Ex 23:6
15. Deut 1:16-17
16. Lev 24:19
17. Ex 21:23-25
18. Ex 21
19. Ex 21:27
20. Amos 5:21-24
21. Hos 6:6
22. Mic 6:7-8
23. Isa 1:11,13,14,23
24. Prov 21:3
25. Lk 11:42
26. Mk 12:33
27. Lk 4:16-19
28. Mt 25:31-40

Part Three
Interpreting the Bible for Today

1. Ideas Change

The bible is not a book of unchanging fixed ideas. The bible constantly updates many of "God's rules" within itself. Jesus radically updates the interpretation of many Old Testament laws and traditions. Change and debate are integral features of the bible. In asking questions and challenging existing beliefs, we continue in the biblical tradition.

Sometimes we have to abandon old ideas. Beliefs about what is morally right or socially acceptable change all the time and vary according to race, religion and culture. In Britain and other western countries, many ideas have changed in recent years. It is not so long ago that respectable British citizens thought slavery was acceptable. It is not so long ago that we thought capital punishment was advisable. It is not so long ago that corporal punishment was the accepted norm. It is not so long ago that we had a male-dominated society where women could not vote and were expected to leave paid work when they married. It is not so long ago that servants were expected to show deference to their employers and not aspire to change their social status. It is not so long ago that having a baby outside of marriage was considered a disgrace. It is not so long ago that same-sex relationships were illegal. It is not so long ago that few provisions were made for people with disabilities. It is not so long ago that it was common to have little respect for people of other faiths.

Many of these things were accepted as a normal part of everyday life in bible times. That was the accepted belief and social system in the culture of the time. According to the Old Testament, these attitudes were correct and approved by God. There are, of course, many areas of the world where they all still apply. In western Christian countries, the majority of people have already decided that we don't need to follow the bible on these issues. For example, we agree that the practice of slavery and all kinds of discrimination are unacceptable. By implication, this means we no longer regard them as God's rules. We can understand how and why people believed these things two to three thousand years ago, living as they did in very different circumstances, but our ideas have moved on, although we still have a long way to go to be anywhere near the society God would like. Perhaps in some future time Christians will say, "Well, that was how people saw things in the twenty-first century. We know better now."

Can we really believe that God instituted all the attitudes to people and society that we see in the early Old Testament? Did God ever really want all those burnt animals? Did he really want to exclude disabled people? Did he really decree that a woman should marry the man who raped her? We could go on to make a long list. If we can say people were mistaken about the above issues, why can't we say that they were equally mistaken about God requiring war and violence and horrific punishments? What is the difference? Most of the rules and practices we have abandoned were, according to the way the bible is written, ordained by God. These are not God's rules. They are the rules devised by ancient people to suit the needs of their day. Many were advanced for their time and they saw the need to keep reviewing them as conditions and beliefs evolved.

The bible constantly updates "God's rules" within itself. Jesus radically updates the interpretation of many Old Testament laws and traditions. The Jewish custom, established before the time of Christ, was to have constant debates, discussions and suggestions about the Scriptures, which involved thoughts and interpretations that went beyond the actual texts. In this way, they explored different possible meanings. A story in the Talmud (a later collection of Jewish ideas) records that the angels wished to sing a song of triumph over the division of the Red Sea. God silences them with the question, "My creatures are drowning and you wish to sing a song?"[1] This shows that there was always some unease about the deaths supposedly caused by God and sympathy for the victims. God is the same yesterday, today and tomorrow. He does not change his values. He inspires forward-looking people to move humanity in the right direction as he has always done and always will. We need to pray for his voice to be heard and to be part of that change where it is needed.

Some people seem to think that we should detach our common sense and God-given brains, intelligence and reasoning powers when we open a bible and accept things we would not accept in other areas of our lives. The bible may have an extra dimension above the ordinary but that will not be lost if we explore it with all our abilities in focus.

If we can put our preconceived ideas to one side and look at what we are reading objectively, it becomes clear that the following things are true:

- The bible does not speak with one voice.
- It contains vastly different and contrasting views about the nature of God.
- The writers disagree about what God wants.
- God's own instructions are said to change and contradict one another.
- There are contradictions in events that cannot be harmonised.
- There are fact-statements that are wrong.

These factors need not be seen in a negative light. Again we have a choice. They can be used to discredit the bible or help to explain how the bible is what it is and how it came into being. The bible does not claim to be without error. It shows ideas changing and developing over time. As was said before, it is a very human book which God adopts and uses. We can find God among the human discrepancies displayed in the bible, just as we can find him in the great array of people we meet in everyday life whom God uses.

Notes
1. Talmud, Megillah 10b and Sanhedrin 39b.

2. Why Read the Old Testament?

Much of the Old Testament, if misunderstood, can give a very distorted and dangerous image of God, so why should we continue to read it? There are a number of good reasons.

The New Testament contains hundreds of references to the Old Testament. There are many direct quotations and constant allusions to laws, customs, events and characters from the past. Having some knowledge of these makes it much easier to understand the New Testament. Many parables and events would have important underlying significance to Jesus' contemporaries.

The New Testament writers saw Jesus as the culmination of the Old Testament story of God and his People. He was the promised Messiah who would establish the Kingdom of God. The Israelites had been chosen to bring a knowledge of the love of the true God to the world. This was where God had chosen to be born as a human being and to make himself known. Jesus is part two of the story. The Old Testament is part one. The Gospel writers believed that the Old Testament contained many promises and predictions about the coming of Jesus. The ones cited are not obviously about Jesus and are often taken out of their original context, which clearly referred to something else that was happening at the time of writing. However, many Christians then and since have found them convincing. For instance, we can see a picture of Jesus in much of Isaiah's description of the suffering servant.[1] According to Luke,[2] Jesus met two followers walking home to a village called Emmaus after his resurrection. They did not at first recognise him. "Beginning with Moses and all the prophets, he interpreted to them the things about himself in all the scriptures." Their reaction after Jesus had left them is, "Were not our hearts burning within us while he was talking and opening up the scriptures to us?" I join the queue of many people who would love to know what Jesus said!

Jesus and his twelve disciples were Jews. They lived and grew up in a culture with the Old Testament as their "bible." When New Testament writers refer to "the Scriptures" they mean the Old Testament. Its laws, customs and traditions permeated everyday life. It was part of who they were as people and how they identified themselves. The early Jewish followers of Jesus did not stop being Jews. They did not see themselves as starting a new religion. The Old Testament was still their sacred text. Jesus was a real human being, brought up in this culture and belief system. His parents followed the traditional practices. According to Luke, he was "circumcised on the eighth day" (Luke 2:21) and presented in the Temple as a baby, as the law required. "They offered a sacrifice according to what is stated in the law of the Lord, a pair of turtle doves or two young pigeons."[3] His family made the journey from Nazareth to Jerusalem every year for the feast of the Passover. When Jesus was twelve he was accidentally left behind and was found in the Temple eager to learn from the teachers there.[4]

The gospel writers, especially Matthew, often refer to the Old Testament, and in his ministry and teaching, Jesus constantly quotes the Old Testament himself or refers to events from it. The texts he has grown up with and probably learned by heart, naturally come to mind. Jesus' hearers would have recognised and understood these references. They gave particular meaning and emphasis which is easy to miss. Many of these are puzzling to readers today if we know nothing of their origin. For instance, the "I Am" sayings of St John recall the name of

God given to Moses from the burning bush.[5] The expressive and cherished symbolism of Jesus as the Good Shepherd, the True Vine, the Lamb of God or the Water and Bread of life, all have resonances in the Old Testament stories. Jesus comes into conflict with the religious authorities when his teaching and actions challenge the established Old Testament laws concerning Sabbath observance, ritual cleanliness and sacrifice which were considered major marks of the Jewish faith. These are prescribed in detail in Exodus, Leviticus and Deuteronomy. Jesus quotes the Old Testament himself. He radically updates many established laws. "You have heard that it was said… but I say to you"[6] and his condemnation of hypocritical and uncaring attitudes[7] reflect many of the Old Testament prophets. "This people honours me with their lips but their hearts are far from me: in vain do they worship me, teaching human precepts as doctrines."[8]

Jesus' replies to the devil after each of the three temptations,[9] come from Deuteronomy. Many gospel stories take on more significance when we can reflect back to Old Testament events, rules and customs. The parable of the Good Samaritan becomes much more radical if we know that Jews and Samaritans hated each other for long-standing historical reasons and that the strict purity laws meant that the priest and Levite would not be able to carry out their duties in the Temple if they had been made "unclean" by touching the injured or possibly dead man. As in many other instances, Jesus is treading on sensitive toes!

Matthew is particularly anxious to connect Jesus with the Old Testament in order to convince the Jewish people that he is indeed the promised messiah. Events in Jesus' life remind him of (or are matched with) well-known Old

Testament stories and sayings. His record of Herod's ordered slaughter of the babies in Bethlehem designed to kill Jesus,[10] would immediately bring to mind the birth of Moses and the mass killing of Israelite children ordered by Pharaoh at that time.[11] Jesus spends forty days in the wilderness, matching the forty years that the Israelites lived in the wilderness before entering the "Promised Land." Jesus goes "up the mountain"[12] to teach what we now call the Sermon on the Mount. This connects with Moses going up the mountain to receive the Ten Commandments. (Exodus 19:20)

So there are many ways in which our knowledge of the Old Testament enhances our understanding of the New Testament but there are other reasons for reading it.

Let's be positive
In part one, we saw that there is a large amount of violence in the Old Testament which does not represent the true character of God and that we cannot rely on many of its characters as role models for moral guidance but there is also a positive side which should not be overlooked. The Old Testament also has many inspiring stories and passages.

In the prophets we find exhortations to be a caring and peaceful society from which our twenty-first century world would do well to take advice. There are dreams of a more peaceful existence in an idyllic future in which enemies will be no more and:

"They will not hurt or destroy on all my holy mountain."[13]

"They shall beat their swords into ploughshares, and their spears into pruning hooks; nation shall not lift up sword against nation, neither shall they learn war anymore."[14]

Even violence in nature is to come to an end. The animals will all be herbivores so lion, lamb, wolf and calf can live side by side and children can play with what were poisonous snakes. This passage looks back to the creation story in Genesis where people and animals were created to be vegetarians![15]

Personal guidance
Many Christians find spiritual strength and guidance through a great variety of Old Testament passages. The Psalms are very popular. The twenty-third psalm is probably one of the best-known passages of the bible. But be warned; they are also full of desire for violence and revenge. The sagas and responses to God include a whole range of human experiences with which people of all times can identify. They can speak to those in similar situations, especially of suffering and persecution. They tell us that we are allowed to question God and to voice our doubts and negative feelings.

There are numerous promises which we can take for ourselves and our guidance, although they were originally written for a specific person or situation in the distant past. A favourite is: "For surely I know the plans I have for you, says the Lord, plans for your welfare and not to harm you, to give you a future with hope. Then when you call upon me and come and pray to me, I will hear you. When you search for me you will find me; if you seek me with all your heart." Jeremiah 29:11

Isaiah 43:1 is another: "I have called you by name and you are mine."

There are numerous passages of hope and encouragement such as, "... those who wait for the Lord shall renew their strength, they shall mount up with wings like eagles, they shall run and not be weary, they shall walk and not faint."[16]

Everything has a particular meaning in its context and we should be aware of what that is but there are times when a passage can speak to us personally outside of that context.

I referred in the first chapter to a personal example. Our class were to have the opportunity of taking turns to read a scripture lesson in the school assembly. It was optional and being a shy child who always avoided being the centre of attention, I intended to say no. However, when the time came, for a reason I could not explain at the time, I felt that I should say yes. The reading was from the first chapter of Joshua and ended "Be strong and courageous; do not be frightened or dismayed, for the Lord your God is with you wherever you go." I heard that as a message for me. I learned that God could help me do things I found difficult and decided that I should make an effort to be less shy. At that point, I had not read the book of Joshua and did not know what horrors it contained! So despite their context, those words spoke to me at that time and ultimately influenced the career I chose to follow as a teacher.

What uses might difficult violent passages have? They can certainly be examples of what not to do and how not to behave. They can be a warning about our personal or group behaviour. Are we selfish or jealous or tempted to cheat or take revenge or hold a grudge? They can help us to think carefully about who we see as role models. Might we be wrong about what we think God is saying to us today, as the bible characters must sometimes have been? The examples of extreme violence supposedly carried out by God, should alert us to the fact that we should not believe everything the bible says about the character of God. It

Disowning the Violence

often shows what people thought, rather than what God is really like. The message of Jesus in the bible leads us to believe that anything that harms other people cannot be from God.

Over the centuries, the stories of the bible have also been used as allegories or been given spiritual interpretations. For example, the constant Old Testament problem of worshipping other gods can come to stand for things in our lives today which tempt us away from God. They can remind us not to adopt current values which may be popular but are morally wrong. The need for respect for all people and care for those in difficult circumstances is every bit as much an issue now as it was for the Israelites. War is still common and human ingenuity and technology have invented more hideous ways to kill. All kinds of persecution fill our news channels and much is never seen. Do we work for peace and human rights? As we read bible stories "against the grain" and see the events from the point of view of the victims, we can consider the feelings of others in contemporary situations and see the comparisons in the twenty-first century world. Abuse of power, exploitation, oppression and extermination of minorities is still going on. There is plenty of modern-day slavery and discrimination. Most of the Old Testament horrors are still around, though in different circumstances. We must not allow the misuse of the bible to condone immoral and outdated beliefs and practices.

Whilst not denying the horrors of some aspects of the Old Testament, we can nevertheless find much to learn from its positive aspects and it is particularly valuable in helping us better understand many aspects of the New Testament.

We can all contribute towards making our world a

better place by disowning the violent acts supposedly attributed to God and affirming his real values as shown in Jesus.

Notes
1. Isa 53
2. Lk 24:25-27
3. Lk 2:22
4. Lk 2:41
5. Ex 3:14
6. Mt 5
7. e.g. Mt 15
8. Isa 29:13
9. Mt 4
10. Mt 2:16-18
11. Ex 1:22
12. Mt 5:1
13. Isa 11:9
14. Isa 2:4
15. Isa 11:6-9, 65:25, Gen 1:29-30
16. Isa 40:31

3. The Next Generation

If we are serious about disowning the violence attributed to God and see the bible as an evolving collection of many people's beliefs, we must think very carefully about how we teach our children. Look along the shelves of a bookshop. How many children's bibles and bible story books have Noah's ark on the front cover? Is this really the first story we want to tell our children? "God was angry and decided to destroy the world" OK, so we play down that bit... and we don't dwell on the horrific picture of everyone struggling and drowning which would certainly get an 18+ certificate on the films if portrayed realistically. If the children listening had lived at the time of Noah, they would have been included in the destruction!

So why is the story so popular? Well of course, children love animals – and the art and craft possibilities are endless. I sometimes wonder how much the choice of bible story really has to do with God.

Generations of Sunday school teachers (and writers, illustrators, publishers, film-makers and, in the case of Noah's ark, toy manufacturers) have loved Old Testament stories. They are dramatic and exciting, making it easy to keep children's attention and interest. But what impression of God are they giving? Before presenting anything to children we should be asking: "What is the reason for teaching this? What are we learning about God and/or ourselves?" Can we be unintentionally giving the wrong impression?

All this has considerable implications for the way we teach our children. We must be very careful when we tell children Old Testament stories that we avoid passing on an impression of God that has been subsequently transformed by Jesus. Any teacher will tell you that it is harder to

The Next Generation

unlearn bad habits and correct misinformation than to start from scratch. With this in mind, how we start passing on bible knowledge is of vital importance. Unfortunately, bible stories have tended to be taught in a way that assumes they are all *literally* true. The danger is that young people either develop narrow literal beliefs or throw the whole bible out along with Father Christmas, the Easter bunny and the tooth fairy. They need to grow up with a realistic and intelligent approach to the bible, which grows with them and makes sense alongside their other areas of learning and experience.

There seems to be a common belief among Christians that it is important for children to know the Old Testament bible stories, so it is considered appropriate to tell sanitised versions of the horror stories which depict God as a ruthless killer. But these sanitised versions are giving a distorted impression of the actual bible content and intention of the authors. They infer that what happens is good and literally true. For instance it can be great fun to act out the dramatic fall of the walls of Jericho but **w***hy are the walls falling down?* They are falling down so that the Israelites can charge in and murder the inhabitants of an entire town! This is one whole story of which the destruction of the walls is an integral and significant part. By praising the first part of the story we, in effect, endorse the second: genocide planned and ordered by God! It's like biting into an apple that looks good on the outside only to discover that the inside is full of worms. Many who enjoyed the Sunday school stories have discovered the worms in later life with devastating results!

As already explained, I gave up on the Old Testament after reading Jericho and other similar stories. I was by no means alone in my reaction. I was fortunate not to have given up on God at the same time but many other people have. God's horrific violence in the Old Testament is a common reason given for being unable to believe in a loving God.

How often do our readings leave out the worst verses? We pretend that they don't exist and don't talk about them. We wish that they did not exist but they do. They make us feel uncomfortable and may niggle at our faith but we dare not ask the questions, perhaps because of the seeming impossibility of finding an answer. We push it to one side and persuade ourselves that the sanitised version is the truth.

Struggling with these dark issues is something we must face and resolve as adults. They are not innocent stories for children. Presenting them as something great and praiseworthy that God has done is wrong. The God we see in Jesus would never have condoned such violent actions. We need to disbelieve the whole story, not just hide a part of it.

To simply tell many Old Testament stories at face value can give an impression of a God who is unfair, harsh, cruel, vengeful or a military tyrant, zapping those who displease him. Joshua, Gideon, Samson, David, etc., are portrayed as God inspired military heroes. Jesus contradicted the common idea, still believed by many in his time, that the Messiah would be just such a leader.

These stories clearly show God having favourites. He protects some and destroys others and traditionally this is presented as something good. Jesus shows this to be untrue; he lived and died for everyone.

In part one, chapter three, we thought about imagining what the story would look like from the victim's point of view. We must not fall into the trap of treating immoral behaviour as virtuous. We should acknowledge that some of the bible's "heroes" were cheats, liars, and murderers. From the Philistine perspective, Samson was a suicide bomber. Before that, he burned cornfields in an act of revenge which was also extremely cruel to animals, behaved very foolishly and irresponsibly in telling Delilah the secret of his strength and is a fairly all round example of how not to behave! (Judges 15/16)

Many bible "heroes" are not good role models. Jacob is a revered figure but he gained his blessing as first born son by bullying his brother and tricking his dying father. The tables were turned when he was tricked into marrying Leah instead of Rachel but Jacob then spectacularly swindled his father-in-law in dividing the flocks of sheep and goats. He showed great lack of judgement in the way he favoured Joseph above his other children. (Gen 25/27/30/37)

The God we see in Jesus is willing to use flawed people who make mistakes but would not have seen such examples of bad behaviour as praiseworthy. The way these Old Testament "heroes" are frequently presented ignores the negative aspects of their behaviour. Many of these characters are only heroes if we accept the image of God as a warrior who sanctions mass murder. This is not what should be conveyed to our children.

"In the spring of the year, the time when kings go out to battle..." (2 Sam. 11:1) makes going to war sound like a natural, normal event; no provocation, not self defence. So many Old Testament stories involve aggression sanctioned, ordered and praised by God.

So it is vitally important that we are aware of what lasting impressions we are (often unconsciously) giving about God. I eventually came to appreciate that there is much to value in the Old Testament, and that knowledge of it is necessary for understanding the New Testament. We need to pass this Old Testament knowledge on to our next generation when they are mature enough, but teaching must be age appropriate. Most Old Testament stories are not suitable for young children. The Old Testament must come with background knowledge if it is not to give a false, unbelievable or inconsistent impression of God. We should constantly compare Old Testament values with those of Jesus. Comparing and discussing the image of God in specific Old and New Testament passages can be a valuable method of teaching this important concept.

Many non-Christians have a caricatured idea of what Christians believe which can give a very distorted picture of God, the bible and the Christian faith in general. We need to make sure that our children's faith includes an intelligent understanding of the bible which enables them to meet the challenges to faith that they may come across in the future. Will they have realistic answers that can satisfy themselves and others? We must confront the difficult issues when young people are mature enough to engage with them and no doubt have questions to ask. Ignoring them is dangerous.

It is vital for a true understanding of Christianity that is faithful to Jesus and therefore to God, that we disown the destructive images of God which belonged to ancient cultures. This must be reflected in what we choose to teach our children and young people.

4. In Summary

"Houston we have a problem," announced the crew of Apollo 13 on its mission to the moon in 1970. Mission control solved the problem with what at first looked like a jumbled collection of assorted objects which would be available to the astronauts. With knowledge, imagination and faith, they put them together to make a life-saving piece of equipment and Apollo 13 returned safely to Earth. This could be a good analogy for the bible.

Try to think of all the accumulated collection of ideas and information we have explored in the previous chapters:

- God inspired ancient people over a period of 1,500 years to record what they believed about God and their experience of their relationship with him.
- This was done within their cultural worldview. Context is crucial in all interpretation and has to be taken into account.
- The bible was written, compiled, edited and translated through a long, complicated and controversial human process.
- Many stories tell us more about the people who wrote them and the belief systems of the time than they tell us about God.
- Truth can be conveyed in many different ways which do not have to be literal or factual. Stories and poems are great teachers. They ignite our imagination and emotions. Figures of speech can be shorthand for the inexpressible.
- There is no one single accurate version of history. Old Testament history is mainly designed to tell one overarching story: the saga of God and his chosen people.
- Historical research of documents outside the bible

and archaeological finds question the reliability of much biblical history which was traditionally viewed as factual. A lot of recounted events may never have happened.
- The bible contains many contradictions, repetitions, mistakes and different opinions. These should not worry us. They are signs of a genuine human record of several thousand years of activity.
- The Old Testament as a whole is not a clear guide to moral behaviour. Many of its characters are flawed, fallible people who often behave very badly. They are not good role models. They portray every human emotion and reaction, both good and bad.
- God can and does use flawed people. He has to; there are no other kind! He must think we are worth the effort; he thought we were worth the human life he lived and died in Jesus.
- We do not find a clear and consistent picture of the nature and attributes of God in the Old Testament. He often appears more like a capricious human with super powers. Yet at other times he shows compassion, patience, mercy and forgiveness. He is also frequently depicted as speaking and acting in ways which are completely incompatible with the nature of God as shown in Jesus. This is particularly true for all the acts of violence that are attributed to him. We should be willing to say, "That can not be true because God would never act in that way."
- Attitudes to women, children, slavery and disability are those of the time and culture. They do not represent God's opinion.
- We should find many Old Testament stories shocking. We should read "against the grain". We

should see the view from "outside the ark" and from inside the besieged city.
- We must ask what image of God we are giving to our children and the rest of the world in the way we use the bible.
- Despite its flaws and problems, God has adopted the bible and speaks to us through its pages. It gives us the life-transforming message of Jesus. It gives us so many purple passages of inspiration for our life and faith in both the Old and New Testaments. We need to read it with realism and with an expectation of being guided by God. These two things are perfectly compatible. God is alive and active in our real world.
- As Christians, we should try to see all life, including the bible, through the lens of Jesus.

5. Conclusion

"God so loved the world that He gave..." Himself, in Jesus, to live and die a truly human life: God emptying himself to become a human being. There can be no greater demonstration of love than this. God is not just a being who loves. His nature is the essence of love: God is what love is. He cannot act in a way that is not loving. That does not mean he is "meek and mild". He can be angry and frustrated, disappointed and sad when people do not act with compassion, justice and forgiveness and do not understand his message. But it does mean that he cannot act with destructive and cruel violence or incite others to do so. This would be totally against the nature of God.

We therefore have to say, whatever other traditional beliefs about scripture it may seem to contradict, God did not order genocide or carry out the multiple acts of violence recounted in many Old Testament Stories.

The bible is invaluable because it brings us the "Good News" of this amazing God who loves us – each one of us – so much. It is in Jesus that we begin to see the depth of this unimaginable love.

But God is not a dictator. He gives us freedom and the ability to choose: freedom to think, freedom to act, freedom to write. God inspired countless people through the centuries to talk, discuss, and later write about their awakening and developing ideas and of a being beyond them and outside their experiences to fully articulate. As their awareness and relationship with God grew, they had to work out what they believed God was like and what he expected of them. This came to them and was expressed through the everyday culture, knowledge and understanding in their place and time. They made mistakes – they were human.

Conclusion

The bible brings us these accumulated experiences of searching for truth and a better understanding of the values and will of God.

We are all on that same journey to try to listen to God, to be aware of our blind spots and prejudices and the influences from our environment and culture, past and present, which get in the way of seeing God as he really is. God has not changed but what we believe about him has, will and should.

Just like Christians today, bible characters did not all agree. Why are we here? How does God act in the world? How will he react if we behave badly? What does he want us to do? The Israelites were trying to work out answers to these questions and we still ask the same questions.

Today, we also have some different questions because we live in a totally different time and place but we still cannot agree on the answers. For example, should Christians be pacifists? What are we supposed to think about same-sex marriage, or abortion or genetic engineering? Why does God appear to cure some people in answer to prayer and not others? Does constantly praying for peace or for uncaring hearts to change, actually do any good? Does God find people parking places or lost objects?

We pray about these issues and come up with different answers. Bible characters came up with different answers to the pressing issues of their day. And it's all in the bible! It does not speak with one voice and the multitude of beliefs cannot all reflect God's opinion. The bible is a record of a search; a search we are all called to join in with. Exploration into God did not end with the formation of the collection of writing we call Scripture. It is an ongoing process.

Believing that God ordered genocide, harsh undeserved punishments and vengeful retaliation has had a big influence on the way people have thought and behaved and still does. It has turned many people away from God and Christianity and will continue to do so. As a teenager, I "threw out" the Old Testament. Many throw out God completely. If God's violence is true, who can blame them? Shall we allow this to keep happening? It is essential that Christians contradict this belief. Militant atheists love to quote the violent images of God. They provide brilliant and easy ammunition with which to ridicule Christian faith. The best way to counteract this is for all Christians to completely and confidently disown the Old Testament's violent image of God and affirm Jesus' message of love, forgiveness and inclusion, in their words and actions. Our religious teaching must convey this message. Our bible studies, our commentaries, our sermons must convey this message. It is vital to project this message to the world at large. God did not behave in the violent way described in the Old Testament. I have suggested a varied combination of factors found in the bible which can build the case to support this position. For some people, this will require a radical rethink of how we view the bible as a whole. We cannot blend the nature of God as shown in Jesus with the God depicted in large sections of the Old Testament. It is not possible. We have to choose. The bible constantly updates its teaching; Jesus consistently updated the Old Testament.

God did not write the bible and does not agree with everything it says but he does adopt it as a particular vehicle for reaching out to his people.

Through the bible God can and does inspire, teach, influence, enable, uplift, encourage, challenge and comfort. We can all use it in this way too. What we must not do is use it to oppress, manipulate, marginalise and exclude people or to perpetuate damaging and offensive images of God.

The authority of the bible comes to us through the message of Jesus in word and action and the "cloud of witnesses" inspired by God over the centuries to affirm his ongoing patient commitment to human beings despite the mess and mistakes we make. We must look at all events and opinions through the lens of Jesus and not be afraid to discount the truth of those which do not fit his image of God, including and perhaps especially, those we read in the bible.

Christians must disown the violence!

Appendix

How is the Bible the "Word of God"?

I have been excited and encouraged by the number of people who have welcomed *Disowning the Violence*. It is evident that many readers have shared my concerns about God's supposed violence and find my book helpful and enlightening. However some who have always believed the bible to be "The Word of God" in a traditional sense, struggle with how to reconcile this with some new ideas they wish to accept.

So what do we mean when we say that the bible is the word of God? The phrase can be interpreted in many different ways. It is an emotive phrase which can imply a whole set of beliefs. When a passage from the bible is read out in church and followed by "This is the word of the Lord" it tends to suggest that God wrote and agrees with what has been read, irrespective of the content.

I believe that there are two separate issues involved in this question:

First, do the words come directly from God? My answer would be no, they are the words of their many and varied human authors.

Secondly, does God influence/speak to people through those words? My answer to this would be, "Yes, without a doubt."

God gave humans free will. We are free to do good or to behave badly and do horrendous things to each other and to the planet. God does not prevent us from doing things he does not like. God allowed and encouraged and inspired people down the ages to record what they believed about him, within their time, knowledge and culture. He did not demand a copy of the manuscript of Exodus, for example, in advance and go through it with a red pen. I hope that

How is the Bible the "Word of God"?

much that has been said throughout this book has already established that God can not possibly agree with everything the bible says because its message can be inconsistent and express contradictory views on many issues.

Do we have the bible God intended us to have, showing us the ongoing history of human response and mistakes? Perhaps. He now surely expects us to interpret that history in the light of the life and teaching of Jesus.

As was said in Part 1, Chapter 1, God did not write the bible but he has adopted it and uses it to communicate with those who look for his guidance. The bible can become the word of God for you as you read it. If you seek to find God in its pages, you will.

What Others Say

In academic circles, the historical accuracy and literal truth of large parts of the Old Testament have been questioned for many decades but this has rarely penetrated to the average church congregation. It used to be hard to find any popular books or commentaries which challenged the literal truth of Exodus or Joshua. The issue of God's violence, if even acknowledged as an issue, was variously explained, excused or accepted but mostly ignored. Gradually more people became dissatisfied with this.

More recently, a number of books have been published that directly address the problem. Most agree that the violent image of God contrasts sharply with the life and message of Jesus. They suggest different ways of dealing with this problem but usually stop short of saying categorically that the Old Testament image of God as a violent warrior cannot be true. I list below some authors who do support this claim.

If you would like to read further on this issue I recommend as a start:

Nick Page. *The Badly Behaved bible: Thinking again about the Story of Scripture* (Hodder and Stoughton, 2019).

Nick Page's book has much more extensive information, ideas and insights, and his lively and often humorous style makes it enjoyable to read. Here are some quotes:

"The bible was written, compiled and translated by humans but God filled it with his presence.... It is God who brings it to life!" p. 28

"Ultimately we are faced with a choice. We can either change our view of the bible or change our view of God as a God of love. I know that many Christians insist on believing both that God is love and that he also ordered the extermination of innocent men, women and children. Personally, that is not a view I am prepared to share." p.231

"If we want to read the bible properly, we must read it through the lens of Jesus Christ. And if one part of the bible says something that conflicts with what Jesus says, well I'm going to listen to Jesus first." p. 234

Peter Enns, *The bible Tells Me So: Why Defending Scripture Has Made Us Unable To Read It.* (Hodder and Stoughton, 2019).

"The bible is an ancient book and we shouldn't be surprised to see it act like one. So seeing God portrayed as a violent tribal warrior is not how God is but how he was understood to be by the ancient Israelites communing with God in their time and place." p.262

"God never told the Israelites to kill the Canaanites. The Israelites believed that God told them to kill the Canaanites." p.69

"The past is a fragile thing. It is never 'just there' waiting for us to press replay…Biblical storytellers recall the past, often the very distant past, not objectively, but purposefully. They wove narratives of the past to give meaning to the present – to persuade, motivate and inspire." p.91

"As for Christians, the gospel has always been the lens through which Israel's stories are read- which means, for Christians, Jesus, not the bible, has the final word." p.82

Eric A. Seibert, *The Violence of Scripture: Overcoming the Old Testament's Troubling Legacy.* (Fortress Press, 2012).

"The premise of this book is simple and straightforward: the bible should never be used to harm others, to inspire, promote, or justify violence ... Violent texts must be confronted honestly and directly... by critiquing the violence in them while still considering how these troubling texts can be used constructively." p.2

"In passage after passage, the use of violence is portrayed as an appropriate way to resolve conflict, punish human wrongdoing, and carry out God's will. Texts like these which condone violence and make it appear respectable and even honourable are especially dangerous for readers who are not wide awake to the designs the texts have on them... I am convinced it is best to regard the Old Testament's description of God's involvement in war as reflective of how people thought about God in a particular historical context – rather than as descriptive of what God actually said and did." p.118

Marcus J. Borg, *Reading the bible Again for the First Time: Taking the bible Seriously but not Literally.* (Harper Collins, 2001).

"I see the bible as a human response to God. Rather than seeing God as scripture's ultimate author, I see the bible as the response of these two ancient communities to their experience of God. As such it contains their stories of God, their perceptions of God's character and will, their prayers to and praise of God, their religious and ethical practices, and their understanding of what faithfulness to God involves.

As the product of these two communities, the bible thus tells us about how *they* saw things, not about how *God* saw things." p.22-23

"Yet because the bible is a human product as well as sacred scripture, the continuing dialogue needs to be a critical conversation. There are parts of the bible we will decide need not or should not be honoured, either because we discern that they were relevant to ancient times but not to our own, or because we discern that they were never the will of God... as an example of each: (1) Paul's counsel about whether it is permissible to eat meat left over from pagan sacrifices was relevant to his time, though not very much if at all to our time. (2) I cannot believe that it was ever God's will that the women and children of one's enemies in war should be slaughtered, to use an example from the Hebrew bible; or that it is God's will that the majority of the earth's population be destroyed at the second coming of Christ, to use an example from the New Testament." p.30+note on p.36

Philip Jenkins, *Laying Down the Sword: Why we can't ignore the bible's violent verses.* (Harper One, Harper Collins, 2011)

"When we read biblical accounts of the unparallelled evils of Israel's enemies, we easily recognise the propaganda that regimes direct against their unpopular minorities. p.111
Acts of racial violence and extermination have complex causes....but the conquest passages were available when commanders wanted to justify

barbaric crimes by presenting them as the divine will." p.142

(Jenkins gives many examples and compares violent passages with those of the Qur'an)

John J. Collins, *Does the bible Justify Violence?* (Fortress Press, 2004)

"The bible has contributed to violence in the world precisely because it has been taken to offer a degree of certitude that transcends human discussion and argumentation. Perhaps the most constructive thing a biblical critic can do towards lessening the contribution of the bible to violence in the world is to show that such certitude is an illusion." E-Book location 235

Derek Flood, *Disarming Scripture*. Metanoia Books 2014

"We all need to learn to read the bible like Jesus did. Scripture is only read right when it is read in a way that leads us to a Jesus-shaped life and a Jesus-shaped understanding of God's heart. The priority of Jesus was not on defending a text. It was on defending people, in particular the victims of religious violence and abuse. Jesus did this even though it meant coming into direct conflict with the religious leaders of his day and their interpretation of Scripture."

Michael Prior, *A Land Flowing with Milk, Honey and people.* Lattey Lecture 1998

Quoted in Walter Brueggemann, *An Introduction to the*

Old Testament. (Westminster John Knox Press 2003)
"the biblical narratives which deal with the promise and gift of land are potentially corrupting in themselves and have in fact contributed to war crimes and crimes against humanity in virtually every colonised region, by providing allegedly divine legitimation for Western colonisers."

Rowan Williams, *Being Christian: Baptism, Bible, Eucharist, Prayer.* SPCK 2014
"If in that story we find accounts of the responses of Israel to God that are shocking or hard to accept, we do not have to work on the assumption that God likes these responses. For instance: many of the early Israelites in the Old Testament clearly thought it was God's will that they should engage in ethnic cleansing – that they should slaughter without mercy the inhabitants of the promised land. For centuries people have asked, 'Does that mean that God orders or approves of genocide?' If he did, that would be so hideously at odds with what the biblical story as a whole seems to say about God. One of the great tragedies and errors of the way people have understood the Bible has been the assumption that what people did in the Old Testament must have been right 'because it's in the Bible'. It has justified violence, enslavement, abuse and suppression of women, murderous prejudice against gay people; it has justified all manor of things we now must as Christians regard as evil ... It is by looking at the story of Jesus, the luminous centre, that we discover how to read the rest of it. Jesus living, dying, raised from the dead, breathing his spirit on his church – it

is in this light that you read the rest of the Bible." p.27-28

Timothy Biles, *Letters to God from a Parish Priest.* (Biles, 1995)

"Lord, I've been reading your Old Testament day after day... It is wonderful to read and I love it. But one mistake I never make. I don't believe it is a picture of You. A picture of Your people, struggling to find You, yes. But a picture of You, no. ... They thought you sent plagues as a punishment, they thought You ordered massacres of the innocent, they thought You were for their nation and against everyone else. They made You into a racist, a bully, a nationalist and a man of War. ... I am so sorry that some readers think it reveals You!"

Bibliography

ANDERSON, Bernhard W. *The Living World of the Old Testament,* Fourth Edition. (Longman, 1988)

BILES, Timothy. *Letters to God from a parish priest.* (Biles, 1995)

BORG, Marcus J. *Reading the Bible Again for the First Time.* (Harper Collins, 2001)

BRETTLER, Mark Zvi, ENNS, Peter & HARRINGTON, Daniel. *The Bible and the Believer: How to Read the Bible Critically and Religiously.* (Oxford University Press, 2012)

BRIGGS, Richard. *Reading the Bible Wisely.* (Cascade Books, 2003)

BRUEGGEMANN, Walter. *An introduction to the Old Testament.* (Westminster John Knox Press, 2003)

BRUEGGEMANN, Walter. *Divine Presence Amid Violence, Contextualising the Book of Joshua.* (Cascade Books, 2009)

CHARPENTIER, Étienne. *How to Read the Old Testament.* (SCM Press Ltd, 1982)

COLLINS, John J. *Does the Bible Justify Violence?* (Fortress Press, 2004)

COPAN, Paul & FLANNAGAN, Matthew. *Did God Really Command Genocide?* (Baker Books, 2014)

COWLES, MERRILL, GARD, & LONGMAN III, *Show them No Mercy: Four views on God and Canaanite Genocide.* (Zondervan, 2003)

DRANE, John. *Introducing the Old Testament.* (Lion

Publishing, 1987)

ENNS, Peter. *The Bible Tells Me So.* (Hodder and Stoughton, 2019)

ENNS, Peter. *Inspiration and Incarnation.* (Baker Academic Publishing, 2005)

ENNS, Peter & Mohier, R. Albert. *Biblical Inerrancy: Five Views.* (Zondervan, 2013)

FLOOD, Derek. *Disarming Scripture.* (Metanoia Books, 2014)

HOLLADAY, William L. *Long Ago God Spoke: How Christians May Hear the Old Testament Today.* (Fortress Press ,1995)

JENKINS, Philip. *Laying Down the Sword.* (Harper Collins, 2011)

LOVEDAY, Simon. *The Bible for Grown Ups.* (Icon Books, 2016)

PAGE, Nick. *The Badly Behaved Bible: Thinking Again About the Story of Scripture.* (Hodder & Stoughton, 2019)

PAYNTER, Helen. *God of Violence Yesterday God of Love Today?* (Bible Reading Fellowship, 2019)

SEIBERT, Eric. *The Violence of Scripture.* (Fortress Press, 2012)

TAYLOR, Simon J. *How to Read the Bible Without Switching Off your Brain.* (SPCK, 2015)

WARD, Keith. *What the Bible Really Teaches: A Challenge for Fundamentalists.* (SPCK, 2004)

WILLIAMS, Rowan. *Being Christian: Baptism, Bible, Eucharist, Prayer.* (SPCK, 2014)

WRIGHT, Tom. *Scripture and the Authority of God.* (SPCK, 2013)

ALSO AVAILABLE FROM THE LISTENING PEOPLE

Adventures with God

TREVOR STUBBS

Are you curious about God? Could it be that there is a real Creator who is offering us Light, Life and Love with capital 'Ls'? If so, how do we find Him (or Her)?

Here are eleven ideas of places we might begin. With suggested bible readings and questions to think about, this little book can be used by one person alone or form the basis of a group study.

> All proceeds from this book are used to aid street children in South Sudan

www.ingramcontent.com/pod-product-compliance
Lightning Source LLC
Chambersburg PA
CBHW072055110526
44590CB00018B/3181